Berkshires
Past and Present

Mary L. Martin & E. Ashley Rooney

Schiffer Publishing Ltd
4880 Lower Valley Road, Atglen, Pennsylvania 19310
Printed in China

Acknowledgments

The Berkshire Hills region is so beautiful, so peaceful, that I am delighted to write about this area. Then there are the people who know the region such as Nick Noyes, the Public Relations Director of the Berkshire Visitors Bureau, who was a tremendous asset to this project. I also met some great collectors such as Geoffrey H. Goldberg, Bob Romeo, and Kevin Sprague, and many other Berkshire lovers sent wonderful postcards.

In this book, I have included some of the Native American legends of the area that my *Berkshire Ghosts, Legends & Lore* (2007) contained among other stories.

Mountain Scene on Title Page Courtesy of D. Peter Lund

Other Schiffer Books by Mary Martin and E. Ashley Rooney
Boston, Past and Present, 978-0-7643-3058-2, $24.99
Lexington to Concord: The Road to Independence in Postcards, 978-0-7643-2698-1, $24.95
Greetings from Cambridge, Massachusetts, 978-0-7643-2810-7, $24.95

Other Schiffer Books on Related Subjects
Cape Cod Memories: An Illustrated History in Postcards, 0-7643-2389-x, $19.95
Birds of Cape Cod & the Islands in Postcards, 0-76432448-9, $14.95
Cottages of Oak Bluffs: 20 Postcards, 978-0-7643-2683-7, $9.95

Library of Congress Control Number: 2008942817

Designed by Bruce Waters
Type set in Eras BT
ISBN: 978-0-7643-3133-6
Printed in China

Schiffer Books are available at special discounts for bulk purchases for sales promotions or premiums. Special editions, including personalized covers, corporate imprints, and excerpts can be created in large quantities for special needs. For more information contact the publisher:

Published by Schiffer Publishing Ltd.
4880 Lower Valley Road
Atglen, PA 19310
Phone: (610) 593-1777; Fax: (610) 593-2002
E-mail: Info@schifferbooks.com

For the largest selection of fine reference books on this and related subjects, please visit our web site at:
www.schifferbooks.com
We are always looking for people to write books on new and related subjects. If you have an idea for a book please contact us at the above address.

This book may be purchased from the publisher.
Include $5.00 for shipping.
Please try your bookstore first.
You may write for a free catalog.

In Europe, Schiffer books are distributed by
Bushwood Books
6 Marksbury Ave.
Kew Gardens
Surrey TW9 4JF England
Phone: 44 (0) 20 8392-8585; Fax: 44 (0) 20 8392-9876
E-mail: info@bushwoodbooks.co.uk
Website: www.bushwoodbooks.co.uk
Free postage in the U.K., Europe; air mail at cost.

Printed in China

Contents

Preface: About the Postcard ____ 4

Introduction: The Early Years ____ 5

Chapter One: Sheffield ____ 8

Chapter Two: Great Barrington ____ 13

Chapter Three: Stockbridge ____ 25

Chapter Four: Lenox ____ 36

Chapter Five: Pittsfield ____ 61

Chapter Six: Dalton ____ 92

Chapter Seven: Jacob's Ladder Region ____ 95

Chapter Eight: Rowe ____ 100

Chapter Nine: Mohawk Trail & its Environs ____ 102

Bibliography ____ 127

Index ____ 128

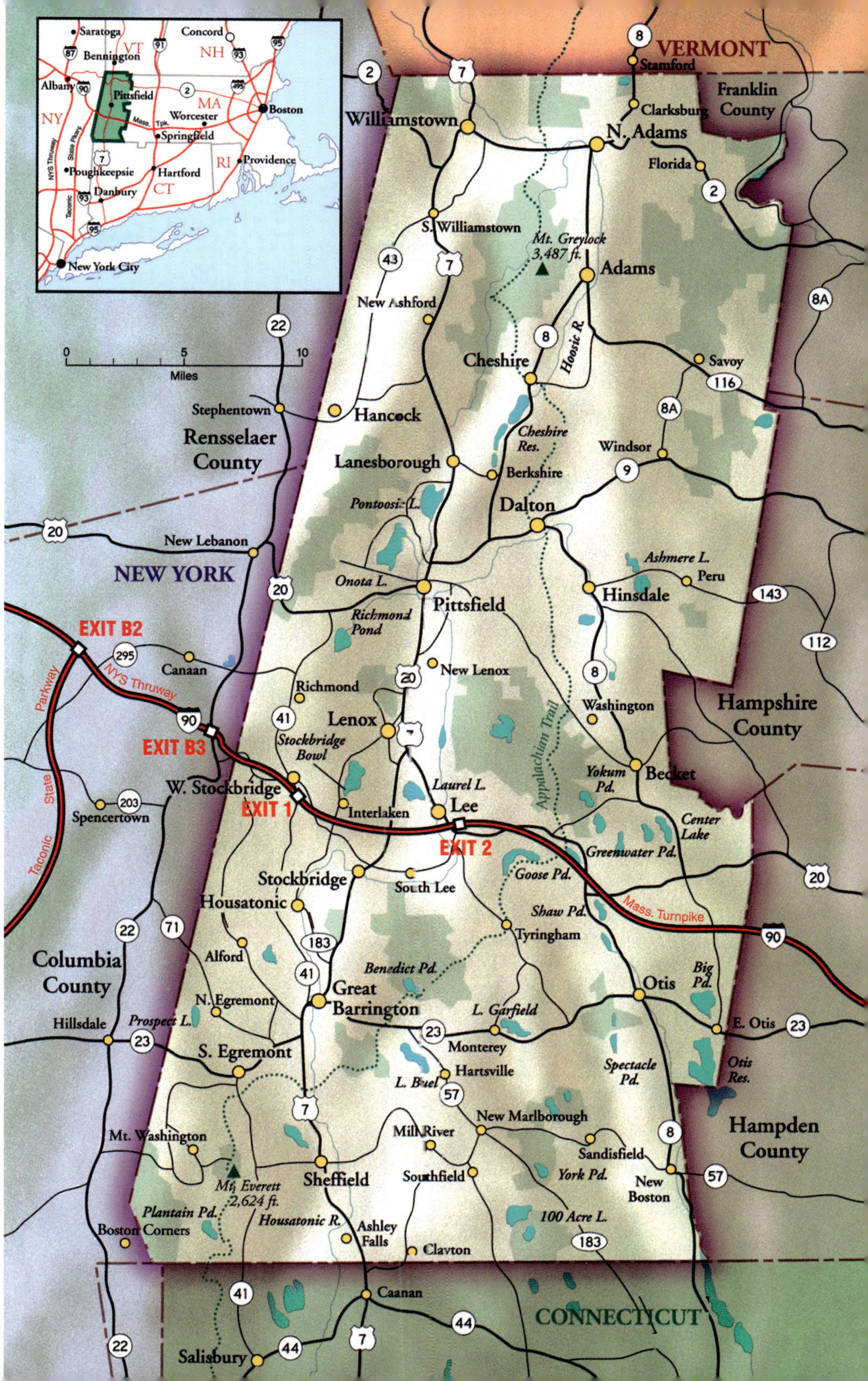

Courtesy of Berkshire Visitors Bureau.

Preface:
About the Postcard

Historic Images Through Postcards

Postcards are said to be the most popular collectible history has ever known. The urge to horde them sprang up with the birth of this means of communication at the turn of the twentieth century and has endured great changes in the printing industry. Today, postcard shows take place every weekend somewhere in the country, or the world, and millions of pieces of ephemera lie in wait for those who collect obscure topics or town views.

Postcards once served as the email of their day. They were the fastest, most popular means of communication beginning in the 1890s in the United States. These timely cards provided a way to send visual scenes through the mail along with brief messages—a way to enchant friends and family with the places travelers visited, to send local scenes, or to share favorite topics of imagery. They even provided the latest breaking news, as images of fires, floods, shipwrecks, and festivals were often available in postcard form within hours of an event. Moreover, mail was delivered to most urban homes in the United States at least twice a day. So someone might send a morning postcard inviting a friend to dinner that evening and receive an RSVP in time to shop for food.

The messages shared and the beautiful scenes featured in *Berkshires, Past and Present* combine to create the timeless appeal of postcards as a collectible. Most importantly, history is recorded with pictures of bygone days, moments in time reflecting an alluring past.

Introduction:

The Early Years

The Berkshire Hills are a wide rolling plateau, stretching some twenty miles, in western Massachusetts. The region is only forty-nine miles long from north to south, extending entirely from Connecticut to Vermont, and twenty-four to twelve miles wide. It encompasses approximately one thousand square miles of forests, fields, hills, rivers, and lakes, which form the headwaters of several rivers.

Originally, the Native Americans inhabited the beautiful Berkshires; the white settlers did not really appear in the area until the early 1700s, long after colonial society was established in eastern Massachusetts and westward in the Hudson River Valley. Both the French and the English claimed the regions and its riches. French troops and their Native American allies attacked villages in the central and northern Berkshires during the French and Indian Wars.

The first English and Dutch settlers established their farms and homesteads in the rolling hills of the southern end of the Berkshires. In 1724, a group from Westfield, Massachusetts, purchased a large area around Great Barrington and Sheffield from the natives; in 1733, Sheffield was incorporated. In 1739, Indian Town became the Town of Stockbridge. Rhoda Hinsdale was the first child born in Lenox in 1751. In 1761, Berkshire County was incorporated, and the Commonwealth auctioned off large parcels of land for settlement. By the 1791 census, 30,291 registered residents dwelled in Berkshire County.

The Berkshire inhabitants played a major role during the War for Independence. At the Berkshire Congress in 1774, local delegates signed a document declaring the principles of separation from Britain, and Lenox residents endorsed a boycott of British goods. In 1776, Berkshire County militia participated in the taking of Fort Ticonderoga; they fought at White Plains in 1776; and, later they were involved at Bennington during Burgoyne's advance from Canada in 1777.

As more white settlers inhabited the region, the relentless pressure of their westward migration displaced the Native Americans. Many had sided with the settlers during the French and Indian Wars: one company served with the famed Rogers Rangers in 1756, and another fought with George Washington at White Plains twenty years later. Ultimately, they were forced to move west, eventually settling in Wisconsin and Oklahoma.

Different forces led to development in the Berkshire region. The northern Berkshire towns had abundant waterpower, but the Berkshire Mountains were a formidable barrier to commerce. With the advent of the railroad and the development of the Hoosac Tunnel in the mid-nineteenth century, the towns became known for their booming textile and shoe industries and paper mills. Ultimately, many of these factories were closed, and the area began to focus on its natural beauty and outdoor activities such as hiking, skiing, fishing and camping.

In the southern area, several Berkshire towns became popular with the country's elite as they built what they called "cottages" throughout the pastoral landscape. From the late 1800s to 1920, towns such as Lenox and Stockbridge were summer colonies for the American economic elite from New York and Boston. Bankers, leaders of industry and robber barons, they were the ones with the next innovation or new product that would help transform America to an industrialized nation of international standing. Ultimately, the income tax, World War I and the Great Depression ended what is known as the Gilded Age. Many of these cottages were torn/burned down, became preparatory schools, or were restored as hotels and spas.

Today, the Berkshire region is famous for its cultural institutions such as Tanglewood, Shakespeare & Company, MASS MoCA, and Jacob's Pillow. A multitude of other performing arts venues present dance, theater, and music throughout the season. There are "cottages," lovely gardens, and great inns to visit. The unique galleries, shops, and museums are open year round in the charming small towns. Hikers, campers, and fishermen gravitate to its lakes, mountains, and rivers. As a whole, the region offers peace, tranquility, and wonderful recreational opportunities.

GREETINGS FROM THE BERKSHIRES, MASS.
S-501
FRASHER PHOTO
© CURT TEICH & CO., INC.

In the Berkshires, Headwaters of the

Chapter One:
Sheffield

Originally called Outhotonnook, meaning "over the mountain," Sheffield is the oldest town in Berkshire County, settled in 1725. Chief Konkapot and other Stockbridge Indians are said to have sold the township in 1724 for 460 British pounds, three barrels of cider, and thirty quarts of rum.

Owned by the Trustees of Reservations and listed on the National Register of Historic Places, the Ashley House exemplifies early eighteenth century architecture. Its Colonial period paneling, broad fireplace and staircase, hand carvings, ornaments and decorations date from the eighteenth and early nineteenth centuries. Courtesy of D. Peter Lund.

The Old Parish Church was built in 1760. Constructed in 1790, the Lich Gate of the Episcopal Church offers shelter.

The Spirit of Bash Bish Falls

A long time before the English began exploring North America, a lovely Mohegan woman, called Bash Bish, lived in a village near the falls with her husband and daughter. Everyone liked her because she was such fun to be with — everyone but one, who professed to be her friend. Of course, like many of us who never imagined that we could have an enemy disguised as a friend, Bash Bish didn't realize that her jealous friend planned to hurt her.

One day her friend accused her of having a love affair with a man other than her husband. In front of the tribal council, Bash Bish begged, cried, and pled her innocence, holding out her infant daughter, asking, "How can you accuse me? You're my friend."

"But you are guilty of breaking tribal laws," sneered her enemy, "You deserve to die." The laws of the tribe were harsh, and the village council condemned her to death by water. They planned to tie her in a canoe and launch it upstream.

That morning, the air was cold and still. Even the crowds were quiet, and the small animals scurried deep into the forest. As the Indians tied her into the canoe and placed it into the water, the rays of the sun shone all around her, creating a golden aura, and multihued butterflies rose like winged blessings. The Indians were awe struck. Was Bash Bish a witch? A spirit?

The canoe with her strapped in it plunged over the falls. Downstream, the Indians retrieved the broken canoe, but much to their astonishment her body had disappeared. Later, people said they could see her spirit shimmering in the water, but many people forgot about her unless they had been there the day when the butterflies flew.

An old squaw adopted Bash Bish's baby. She named her White Swan because she was so fair. As she grew, she became more beautiful each day. She was so lovely that the Chief, Black Thunder, picked White Swan as a bride for his son, Whirling Wind. For many months, these two happily roamed the beautiful Berkshire woods while Whirling Wind demonstrated his hunting skills to his lovely bride. He could bring down moose, deer, and even bear with his bow and arrow. She would run along the trail behind her husband. Sometimes she would join him in fishing for salmon and trout. They would sit for hours while he told her about his adventures when the tribe on the warpath. In the evening, they would sit and listen to the whispering of the pine trees and watch the fireflies flitting through the evening's dusk. Although White Swan and Whirling Wind were devoted to each other, they had one great sadness—she was unable to conceive.

Now, Whirling Wind was Black Thunder's only son and heir. When Black Thunder died, Whirling Wind would be the chief. He also had to have a son and heir. The young couple visited the Medicine Man who brewed many different potions and performed dances by the light of the mystic fire deep in the forest, but still White Swan did not get pregnant.

Finally, Black Thunder announced that Whirling Wind must take another squaw to his wigwam—one that would give him an heir. Reluctantly, Whirling Wind took a second wife. Although White Swan understood the reasons why this must be done, she was not happy. Her glowing smile no longer brightened the wigwam. She no longer happily followed her husband up the trail or sat in the front of his birch bark canoe. Instead, they slowly and silently trod the path to the high rock above the falls. There, she would sit and watch the plummeting waters. Sometimes when Whirling Wind left her at the village, he could hear her talking to the spirit that all the Indians knew lived in the plunging cascade.

One night, when the moon was full, White Swan rose from her couch and left Whirling Wind's wigwam. He watched her go and then quietly followed her, but she was a good deal faster than he. She ran like a deer along the path, over the slippery rocks, to the high rock on which she sat and watched the falls. Whirling Wind called to her as he tried to jump over the treacherous rocks over which she skimmed like the bird for which she had been named. He could hear the water splashing below. Breathless, he arrived at the base of the falls, just as she stepped onto the highest rock above. He was just in time to hear her cry, "Hear I am, Mother; take me into your arms," and she disappeared into the water. The waters roiled briefly and a beautiful white mist rose up. Desperate, Whirling Wind dove after her and succumbed to the tumult.

The Indians found Whirling Wind's battered body. They never found White Swan's body, which, like that of her mother's, disappeared. Some say that the voices of these two women can be heard in the waterfall's gurgling. Others say that they can see White Swan's face, formed by the swirling waters at the base of the falls, looking upward to the spot where she and her husband plunged to their deaths.

Today, the quiet village of Sheffield is known for its pastoral beauty with its broad river valley and mountain vistas. Previously, it was famous for its tobacco farms and marble quarries. Courtesy of D. Peter Lund.

The Ashley Falls area of Sheffield is the site of Bartholomew's Cobble, a 329-acre park owned and managed by the Trustees of Reservations. Named for its two rocky knolls or "cobbles" that rise above the Housatonic River, it has hiking trails and is home to many fern species and woodland wildflowers.

A popular Berkshire tourist stop, Bash Bish Falls has been a favorite subject for painters and photographers since the mid-nineteenth century. Most visitors stay at the lower twin falls and rock-bottomed basin. Only the braver attempt to explore the upper reaches of the multiple falls. Courtesy of Robert D. Evans.

Bash Bish Falls is the highest single-drop waterfall in the Commonwealth. It cascades through a series of gorges surrounded by forest until the water meets a large granite outcrop, which splits it into two fifty-foot cataracts that tumble into a clear green mountain pool. Bash Bish Brook continues through New York State until it finally joins the Hudson River on its way to the Atlantic.

Waterfalls make many sounds. They bubble, slosh, gurgle, chortle, splash, murmur, ripple, and babble. Some say that Bash Bish Falls says its name over and over: "bashbish, bashbish, bashbish." When you visit, see if you can hear it. Courtesy of Robert D. Evans.

Bash Bish Falls is located next to the 4,169-acre Mount Washington State Forest, which offers thirty miles of trails, including the South Taconic Trail and wilderness camping. The Taconics, among the oldest mountains in North America, have been worn low by millions of years of erosion. The Berkshire Hills are part of the range. Courtesy of Birchwood Inn.

Chapter Two:
Great Barrington

First settled in 1726, Great Barrington was named after the village of Great Barrington in Gloucestershire, England. It is known for the first open resistance to British Judiciary and the freeing of the slaves under the Bill of Rights, which led to the abolition of slavery in Massachusetts. In 1774, an estimated 1,500 colonists blocked the royal judges from sitting in court at Great Barrington. With the arrival of the railroad, Great Barrington developed into a Gilded Age resort community for those seeking relief from the heat and pollution of cities. Wealthy families built grand homes or "cottages" here, as others would in Lenox and Stockbridge.

Great Barrington is famous for being the home of W. E. DuBois, a black civil rights activist and the first African-American to earn a doctorate from Harvard University. It's also the site of the first agricultural fair in the nation. In 1886, William Stanley, Jr., demonstrated the use of his AC distribution system to illuminate the streets and offices along Great Barrington's main street. His innovation is commemorated in the monument.

In 1895, Colonel William L. Brown, part owner of the *New York Daily News*, presented Great Barrington with a statue of a newsboy, now a landmark on the western edge of town.

Cottages, Big and Small

Poet and journalist William Cullen Bryant practiced law in Great Barrington from 1816 to 1825. Eventually, he gave up the profession and went on to become an American romantic poet, journalist, and long-time editor of the *New York Evening Post*. An early advocate of American literary nationalism, he is now considered to be very sentimental. For a year after his marriage, he lived in the old house on Taylor Hill, where many of his poems began. One of his poems told the story of the Indian maiden who, forbidden by the laws of her tribe to marry her cousin lover, died instead.

> There was a maid,
> The fairest of the Indian maids, bright-eyed,
> With wealth of raven tresses, a light form,
> And a gay heart. About her cabin-door
> The wide old woods resounded with her song
> And fairy laughter all the summer day.
> She loved her cousin; such a love was deemed,
> By the morality of those stern tribes,
> Incestuous, and she struggled hard and long
> Against her love, and reasoned with her heart,
> As simple Indian maiden might.
>
> -- William Cullen Bryant

The William Cullen Bryant Homestead, his boyhood home, is now a museum and a National Historic Landmark.

In 1908, William Hall Walker, one of the largest stockholders of Kodak, bought Brookside because William Stanley was bankrupt. Eventually, it, like many of the Berkshire cottages, found other uses.

The seven turrets and blue dolomite exterior of Searles Castle, also known as Barrington House, have towered over Great Barrington for more than 120 years. Great Barrington was Mary Francis Sherwood Hopkins' hometown. A wealthy widow, she had hired Stanford White to design her a summer cottage; her former decorator had been Herter Brothers, where interior designer Edward Searles worked. She developed a great affection for Edward and replaced Architect Stanford White with Henry Vaughan, who was more amenable to Edward's suggestions. In 1887, she and Edward married; she was twenty-two years older than he was.

Hills and Dales

The castle required three years, millions of dollars, and a private railroad to bring the marble used from the quarry. The result was forty rooms, one of which once contained a pipe organ and served as a mini-concert hall. It has over 60,000 square feet of floor space, thirty-six fireplaces in the French chateau style, and many balconies. Its grounds include a T-shape lagoon, tennis courts, and a garden temple guarded by two marble sphinx sculptures. Edward and Mary enjoyed it until her death — four years later. Although many of the treasures of the house were removed by Mr. Searles or subsequent owners, the house is still fascinating. Over the years, it has been a private school, conference center, and cultural attraction.

Great Barrington has a 503-acre Monument Mountain Reservation. The summit offers panoramic views of Southern Berkshire County, and three miles of trails lead through a white pine and oak forest.

Legend of the Monument Mountain

One legend says a Stockbridge Indian maiden married a brave from another tribe, breaking the tribe's code. Her tribe condemned her, as many another had been condemned, to jump or to be thrown from the mountaintop. She refused to jump. So some of her tribesmen bound her hands and feet and carried her to the peak of the mountain. At dawn, as the tribe waited on the plain below, they threw the screaming girl off the cliff. But her kicking, screaming body did not clear a gnarled pine that grew from a crevice in the rocky side of the mountain. Instead, she dangled from one of its sturdy branches over the steep rocky ravine. She struggled to release herself from her bonds, trying to find an escape from her awful death on the rocks below, but without success. Sometimes, she cried out, and sometimes she just hung there, swaying on the branch. Those who had been waiting to see her die began to believe that they had condemned her unjustly.

A low-lying fog turned everything gray. The mountain brooded in the soft mist. The grim-faced braves of the tribe gathered around the council fire to decide what their next steps would be. Obviously, the spirits had disagreed with the sentence imposed on the girl. Some held that the punishment was fixed and nothing could alter it. Others felt that it still could be changed. As they argued, the heavens answered them.

Thunderclouds blanketed the skies. Lighting flashed. Thunder echoed up and down the valley. As the Indians watched to see what would happen, a ball of fire descended through the clouds, enveloping both the tree and the girl. The flames paused for an instant. Then, flickering hard, they rose upward, cradling the beautiful Indian maiden in their hot sling. Higher and higher, this strange hammock rose, until it disappeared into the thunderheads.

People say that no Indian travels through the Monument Mountain pass without making a peace offering to the spirits who had saved the Indian girl from death on the rocks at the base of the peak. They cast a stone to the side of the path as they pray. Some believe that the rock cairn, which marks the spot where she lay buried, gives the mountain its name—Mountain of the Monument.

The 1,642-foot Monument Mountain provides a sweeping view. Nathaniel Hawthorne first met Herman Melville on August 5, 1850, when they enjoyed a well-chronicled picnic hike up Monument Mountain. A thunderstorm forced them to seek refuge in a cave where a vigorous discussion ensued, inspiring ideas for Melville's new book, ***Moby Dick*****.**

Devil's Pulpit, Monument Mountain,
Great Barrington, Mass.

Old man of Monument Mountain, Great Barrington, Mass.
We are located at Monterey. 10 miles
from anywhere. The air is good
There are 8 pigs who follow me
all about like puppies.

Life in the outdoors is special in Great Barrington.

Gibson's Grove, Lake Buel, near Great Barrington, Mass. 94
4A536

A Berkshire I
Rockdale, Great Barrington, Mass.

BROOKLYN BRIDGE
GREAT BARRINGTON, MASS.

Bridge and Indian Fordway Tablet, Great Barrington, Mass.

TWENTY RODS NORTH
OF THIS STONE WAS THE
OLD INDIAN FORDWAY
ON THE MIDDLE TRAIL FROM
WESTFIELD TO THE
HUDSON RIVER
NEAR BY WAS THE SITE OF THE
GREAT WIGWAM WHERE
MAJOR JOHN TALCOTT
OVERTOOK AND DISPERSED A
PARTY OF INDIANS AUGUST 1676
ERECTED 1904
Copyright 1905 by the Rotograph Co.
5254 Indian Fordway Monument, Great Barrington, Mass.
Some more of your friends.
You will remember them. Ed-

THE LITTLE RED BRIDGE,
GREAT BARRINGTON, MASS.

Inns

Oakwood Inn, Great Barrington, Mass., in the Berkshires

Great Barrington, Mass. Berkshire Inn.

Hotel Miller, Great Barrington, Mass.

BERKSHIRE INN, GREAT BARRINGTON, MASS. 42

Chapter Three:
Stockbridge

The Berkshires are world renown for the charming valley villages of Stockbridge and Lenox. Today, these two towns are famous resorts. In the early eighteenth century, they were the home of the Mohegans. As the white settlers busily established themselves as farmers on the lush Berkshire land, a far-sighted Mohegan chief, Konkapot, decided if he couldn't fight them, he'd join them. His tribe would become Christian and learn to write and read English! After negotiations, the Puritans responded by sending the young minister John Sergeant, a gentle, popular Yale tutor from Newark, New Jersey. He cheerfully admitted that he would give up the pleasures of life at Yale to become the missionary pastor of the new Indian parish to be organized in the remote Berkshires.

The young earnest Yale graduate was instantly successful, probably because of his immersion into the Indian way of life. He preached, baptized, and married. No longer would the Mohegans be just hunters and gatherers, they would emulate the colonial farmers and lead settled, regulated colonial lives. To enhance the success of the missionary enterprise, Indian Town was chartered in 1737 and incorporated in 1739 as the Town of Stockbridge. From then on, its inhabitants were known as Stockbridge Indians.

Sergeant's vision of incorporating the colonial way of life with the Indian culture appeared to have been achieved. Even the elective offices of the new town were shared among the colonials and the natives. The saintly Sergeant married high-spirited Abigail Williams, daughter of Ephraim Williams, one of the white settlers. The house that Sergeant built her in 1739, preserved today as Mission House, was quite grand for the time. The paneled doorway with its elaborate woodworking was carved in Connecticut and dragged by oxen over fifty miles of rugged terrain. She maintained the household and raised their children, and he concentrated on converting the Indians and turning them into "civil, industrious, and polished people."

Over the years, the Indians built English houses along a "street" running east and west through the center of town. The trees were cleared, and the church at one end of town was surrounded by the town green and bordered by the graveyard. Then Konkapot and Sergeant died. With Sergeant's death, the Indians lost their champion, and the terms of their agreement were increasingly violated. Although the Indians and the English were supposed to be equal, the ever-increasing colonial population and their influence overwhelmed the Indians. Unscrupulous whites began to seize land that was promised to the Indians in perpetuity. Among them was Sergeant's father-in-law, Ephraim Williams. General Joseph Dwight, who was appointed to manage the town, married the widow Abigail. Under the influence of her father, Ephraim Williams, he became involved in the sale of liquor to the Indians and the mismanagement of the Mission School. The Indians became so dispirited that the school "mysteriously" burned down.

Ultimately, the largely landless Indians left Stockbridge in 1785. After being displaced several times by the relentless pressure of the white settlers' westward migration, they settled, in 1850, on a reservation near Shawano, Wisconsin, where their descendants live today.

When the impoverished Mohegans departed Stockbridge in 1785, they left a small rural village, with dusty streets and meandering livestock. A stagecoach stop, now known as the Red Lion Inn, was established on the road that connected Boston to Albany. Travel at the time was difficult and uncomfortable, and the public house quickly became a popular stopping place for bruised and battered travelers who could stay in one of eight, low ceiling rooms. On cool days, a fire always blazed in the hearth to welcome travelers and townspeople alike, and the innkeeper would hand them a hot punch or rum toddy. Upstairs was a large ballroom, where the big Stockbridge functions occurred. Many country dances took place there; the ladies would sip some cider; the men would indulge in something stronger.

Built in 1739, the house of the Reverend John Sergeant, first missionary to the Stockbridge Indians, is on the Main Street of Stockbridge. Originally, located on Prospect Hill, it was moved in 1927 to Main Street, where it is known as Mission House Museum, a property of the Trustees of Reservations. Mabel Choate contracted with Fletcher Steele, a landscape architect, to work with her on the restoration of the house and the creation of period herb and flower gardens. Courtesy of D. Peter Lund.

Red Lion Inn

The Red Lion Inn played a significant role in the infancy of the United States. In 1774, the Berkshire Convention, presided over by Mark Hopkins and Theodore Sedgwick, voted to no longer consume any British-manufactured goods. The convention met at what was known then as Stockbridge Tavern under the sign of the red lion with the green tail.
Courtesy of The Red Lion Inn, Stockbridge, Massachusetts.

In the winter of 1786, Daniel Shays led a group of more than one hundred armed local farmers and citizens to protest oppressive taxes. Stockbridge was chosen as headquarters for what became known as "Shays Rebellion."
Courtesy of The Red Lion Inn, Stockbridge, Massachusetts.

Fivepresidentshavestayedattheinn:Cleveland,Coolidge,McKinley, Theodore Roosevelt, and Franklin Roosevelt.
Courtesy of The Red Lion Inn, Stockbridge, Massachusetts.

The story is told that when President Coolidge was a candidate for Massachusetts's lieutenant governor, he was left behind at the inn on the eve of a political rally. When found, Coolidge is said to have remarked, "I thought you would come back for me."
Courtesy of The Red Lion Inn, Stockbridge, Massachusetts.

In 1873, Charles H. Plumb and his wife, Mert (for whom the charming Plumb Room was named), bought the inn and began a ninety-year family management dynasty. Developing her image as a voracious antique collector, Aunt Mert published a standing offer of "50 cents for a pitcher, $1.00 for an antique mirror." She would take a horse and buggy and scour the countryside for good antiques. She collected many of the teapots and fine antique furnishings seen in The Red Lion Inn today.
Courtesy of The Red Lion Inn, Stockbridge, Massachusetts.

From The Red Lion Inn's inception until the 1896 fire, its crest was a red lion, representing the crown, waving a green tail indicating its patriot leanings. In 1897, Mr. Treadway unveiled a new crest in the form of a shield. It had a lion; the dates 1773 and 1897, indicating the birth and rebirth of the inn; and a teapot, plate, Franklin stove, highboy, clock, and two large keys, symbolizing the inn's fine collection of antiques, within the body of the shield. The traditional lion that we know today, plump and well fed, to indicate the high quality of food served at the Red Lion, replaced it in the early 1920s.
Courtesy of The Red Lion Inn, Stockbridge, Massachusetts.

In November 1968, the inn was slated for destruction to make room for a gas station. John and Jane Fitzpatrick, the founders of Country Curtains, bought it, planning to use part of it as a home for their growing business. They became so taken with the inn and its history that they decided to continue its operation. The redecorated Red Lion Inn opened for year-around business in 1969. Antique furniture, china, and pewter abound, and the famous teapots are on permanent display. Subsequently, neighboring buildings have been converted into guesthouses.
Courtesy of D. Peter Lund.

A view of the Civil War Monument and the Red Lion Inn.
Courtesy of The Red Lion Inn, Stockbridge, Massachusetts.

Stockbridge Today

By the early nineteenth century, Stockbridge, a rural farming community, was on the main route of the stagecoach line between Boston and Albany; each day four coaches traveled in each direction, making regular stops. As the railroad grew in importance during the mid nineteenth century, the wealthy used it to escape from the increasingly disease- and crime-ridden cities during the summers. Leaving the crowded congested streets, they would enjoy the pastoral scenes and clean air of the country, either in their own summer homes or in one of the many hotels or inns. The railroad came to West Stockbridge in 1842 and to Stockbridge in 1850. Once the railroad chugged into these towns, the villages were discovered.

Stockbridge was a favorite summer resort for the literary, the artistic, and the business leaders of the day. From Longfellow to Edith Wharton, from Daniel Chester French to Aaron Burr, the cultural icons and the political leaders came to enjoy the bucolic scene.

Located in Stockbridge, the Norman Rockwell Museum holds the world's largest and most significant collection of his works, including more than seven hundred paintings, drawings, and studies. It also contains an archive of more than 150,000 photographs, letters, and materials.
Courtesy of Norman Rockwel Museum.

The museum curates innovative exhibitions that explore Rockwell's art and the art of illustration, promoting art appreciation, education, and involvement in visual communication.
Courtesy of Norman Rockwell Museum.

Among the museum's most important holdings is Rockwell's Stockbridge studio building and its contents. Objects in the collection include: the artist's materials and equipment, Rockwell's personal art library, furnishings, decorative objects, mementos, hundreds of prints, and artwork sent by fans and admirers.
Courtesy of the Norman Rockwell Museum. Bonnie Harris. Courtesy of General Electric.

The archway at Chesterwood frames the studio of American Renaissance sculptor Daniel Chester French, where he created the model for the seated Lincoln in the Washington, D.C. memorial, among other famous works.
Courtesy of the Chesterwood Museum, a National Historic Site.

The north light floods the studio where French worked. Visible among his various sculptures are Andromeda, His Majesty, Memory, and George Washington.
Courtesy of the Chesterwood Museum, a National Historic Site.

Architect Henry Bacon, friend and associate of French, designed the stucco and wood home, which commands a broad view of the mountains in the distance. French purchased the property because it was "The best dry view he had ever seen."
Courtesy of the Chesterwood Museum, a National Historic Site.

Nestled in the scenic Berkshire Hills of western Massachusetts, the Berkshire Botanical Garden (BBG) offers visitors a peaceful refuge of natural beauty, stunning display gardens, exciting community events, and informative classes. Courtesy of Berkshire Botanical Garden.

Founded in 1934, the public display gardens are among the oldest in the United States. Courtesy of Berkshire Botanical Garden.

The fifteen-acre botanical garden in Stockbridge contains over 3,000 species and varieties. Courtesy of the Berkshire Botanical Garden.

Chapter Four:
Lenox

Initially, only scattered outposts existed on the Berkshire frontier. Although land in Lenox had been granted to missionary ministers and others, the white settlers did not occupy the region until the mid-eighteenth century. Jonathan and Sarah Hinsdale are thought to be the first white settlers in the area. Their daughter Rhoda was the first child born in Lenox in 1751. Befitting the town's future appeal to tourists, Jonathan Hinsdale opened an inn and general store!

The Lenox colonists took saws and axes to the wilderness, cutting down the great forests, planting fields, and establishing themselves as farmers on land purchased or taken from the Indians. They also developed some industries in the area now known as Lenox Dale, using the local iron ore, quartz sand for glass, and other minerals found throughout the Berkshires. The Town of Lenox became a reality in 1767. Israel Dewey, a large landowner and town leader, held the first town meeting of Lenox on March 1, 1767. The residents constructed a meetinghouse and hired a schoolmaster in 1770.

Lenox joined in the battle of wills between the British Empire and its American colonies. This tension and the division between the patriots and their Tory neighbors intensified the growing rebellion in the area.

Birchwood Inn is sited on the first Lenox residential property deeded by the Massachusetts Bay Colony in 1765. Israel Dewey built the core of the house in 1766-1767, and it served as an inn during that period. The first town meeting was held here on March 11, 1767, the year that the Town of Lenox was incorporated.
Courtesy of Birchwood Inn.

A stone monument in the center of town commemorates Colonel John Paterson, a lawyer who early on had formed a militia of local men. In July 1774, Paterson moved to Lenox and was chosen as a member of the Berkshire Convention. He was made colonel of a regiment he raised in 1775 and was one of the first in the field after the Battle of Lexington. He was made Brigadier General in 1777, commanded West Point in 1780, and was at Major Andre's trial.
Courtesy of Birchwood Inn.

Today's library was once the county courthouse.
Courtesy of Birchwood Inn.

Serge Koussevitzky, the first conductor of the Boston Symphony Orchestra at Tanglewood, is one of the notables buried in the adjacent cemetery.
Courtesy of Church on the Hill.

The Church on the Hill was based on a Bulfinch design. Henry Ward Beech, educator, philosopher, and author, often preached in the original Meeting House (c. 1775).
Courtesy of Church on the Hill.

The Old Curmudgeon

One Tory in Lenox aggravated his neighbors by criticizing everything American — from their customs to their politics. Many of us know people like that today! Although this old Tory was a well-respected member of the gentry, the neighbors could no longer endure his abuse. A committee informed him that he could either swear allegiance to the colonies or be hanged. He declared, "I'd rather be hanged than swear allegiance to THOSE people."

So hanged he was on a ready-made gallows in the street. The patriots let him down after a few minutes, revived him with rum, and offered the oath again.

"Absolutely not," he snarled.

The committee members were troubled. They had assumed that he would forego his loyalty to George III once the cord was put around his neck. After some debate, they hoisted him up again on the gallows. One committee member yanked the noose to show they meant business.

The old curmudgeon hung for some time. When lowered, he gave no sign of life. The committee members were horrified. They didn't want to kill the old fellow; they just wanted him to swear fealty to the American way of life. They worked hard to bring him back. At last, his lungs heaved, the purple faded from his cheeks, his eyes opened, and he gasped, "I'll swear."

The committee members cheered. Hurrying him to the tavern, they seated the former Tory before the fire, and put a glass of punch in his hand. After drinking to George Washington's health, he muttered, "It's a hard way to make Whigs, but it'll do."

Various acts of defiance against the British Crown occurred in Berkshire County. At the Berkshire Congress in 1774, delegates from Lenox and other towns signed a document declaring the principles of separation from Britain in language that the Declaration of Independence echoed later. Lenox residents also drew up a "Covenant" that boycotted British trade.

When war with England began, many Lenox citizens volunteered. The town's military roster displays 231 names. After the war, Berkshire communities soon faced Shay's Rebellion, a clash between New England farmers and their new government. Colonels Paterson and William Walker of Lenox were among the leaders of the troops who fought the ragtag rebels in 1787 in Lee and other locales.

Lenox lobbied to become the county seat and won that distinction over Pittsfield and Great Barrington in 1784. When the court on Main Street was in session, Lenox bustled with activity. The first county jail located on Stockbridge Road was relocated next to the courthouse, at the southeast corner of Main and Housatonic Streets. "Gallows Hill" on West Street was the site of the public-style execution.

By 1800, the town had over a thousand residents. Its iron industry played an important role in the town's economy. In 1805, the congregation constructed a new meetinghouse, which is known as the Church on the Hill. By 1818, the first Episcopal Church was built, which was quickly followed by a Methodist church.

The Gilded Age Cottages

From the late 1800s to 1920, the Berkshires, particularly Lenox with only 1,845 residents and Stockbridge with 2,089 residents, were a summer colony for the American "aristocracy" of the time. During those lovely summer days, these visitors, who often attended the same schools, colleges, clubs, and churches and went to the "best places" in Europe in the season, flocked to Lenox, Stockbridge and, to a lesser degree, Great Barrington to erect summer "cottages."

Captivated by the beauty of the Berkshires and the geographical ease of reaching it, wealthy New Yorkers and Bostonians packed up their families, their household necessities, luggage, horses, and carriages and traveled to their country estates via the New York, New Haven and Hartford Railroad during the summers. The developer of the New York City transit system and President Cleveland's Secretary of the Navy, William C. Whitney, even transported deer, elk, moose, antelope, bison, and other exotic beasts to his summer home and game preserve on October Mountain!

Longfellow, Hawthorne, Melville, Henry James, and Edith Wharton had already found their home here. They were joined by the brightest and the best of the century from Andrew Carnegie to George Westinghouse to Harry Payne Whitney. Then there were the presidents, royalty, diplomats, and bankers.

They all took their leisure very seriously. They came to go to the hunt, the gymkhanas, and the tetherball tournaments; to attend the house parties, the balls, and horse shows; to play golf, tennis, and croquet; to dance, to dine, and to flirt. They came to compete, to impress, and to enjoy this luxurious life.

Each September, before shutting down their cottages for the winters, the moguls marked the end of the season with a parade down Main Street that showcased their prized horses, carriages known as "tubs," and flowers.

Rotch & Tilden designed Belvoir Terrace for Morris Ketchum Jesup, a railway magnate and philanthropist in 1888-1890; Frederick Law Olmstead designed the landscaping. Jesup's study has 10-foot high ceilings and 6½-foot paneling with various secret compartments. Courtesy of Belvoir Terrace and Nancy Goldberg.

John Shepherd purchased the estate in the early 1920s, adding two rooms, enclosing the porch, and installing a slate roof.
Courtesy of Belvoir Terrace and Nancy Goldberg.

Today, Belvoir Terrace, with its great lawn, wooded paths, and imported trees, is a camp devoted to the fine and performing arts.
Courtesy of Belvoir Terrace and Nancy Goldberg.

In 1885-1886, McKim, Mead, & White designed the Choate estate, Naumkeag, which was bequeathed to the Trustees of Reservations who continue to make the house and its gardens open to the public. A National Historic Landmark, the Shingle-style house is famous for its furniture, porcelain, and art collections and its eight acres of terraced gardens and landscaped grounds originally designed by Barrett and expanded by Fletcher Steele.
Courtesy of D. Peter Lund.

Carrere and Hastings, the architects who designed the New York City Public Library, built the G. Foster estate, better known as Bellefontaine, in 1897. Constructed from pale brick and white marble from the Lee quarries, the house was built around an inner court with a long reflecting pool surrounded by a large collection of statuary.
Courtesy of Bob Romeo, Lenox.

After Mr. Foster's death in 1945, the house was sold to the Fathers of Mercy. In February 1949, fire destroyed the interior. The new occupants rebuilt it as the Immaculate Heart of Mary Seminary. It then stood vacant for a number of years before being turned into the Canyon Ranch Spa.

A friend of John Sloane, Robert Paterson acquired a 220-acre Lenox estate called "Highlawn" from the Dorr family. He tore down the original house and built a castle modeled after his mother's ancestral home in Blantyre, Scotland. Construction of this cottage with its towers, turrets, and leaded glass windows began in 1901. At times, the project employed over three hundred people. Eventually, it, like many of the cottages, fell upon hard times.

In 1981, Ann Fitzpatrick Brown reopened Blantyre as a beautiful country hotel, where guests can experience the life and service of a bygone era. Today, the beauty of the Berkshire Hills surrounds this Tudor-style country house hotel with its baronial Main Hall, period pieces, manicured lawns, and magnificent trees.

George and Sarah Morgan employed Rotch & Tilden, prominent Boston architects, to design their Elizabethan Revival summer home. Originally the centerpiece of a twenty-six-acre landscaped garden, the mansion had twenty-eight rooms, including fifteen bedrooms, thirteen bathrooms, a billiard room, and bowling alley. It has gables, stained glass windows, and woodcarvings.

The brick mansion also had the latest modern amenities of the time, including ingeniously ventilated bathrooms, combined gas and electric light fixtures, an elevator, burglar alarms, and central heating.

The property contained several outbuildings, including two gatehouses, a carriage house/stable, and six greenhouses. After the death of the Morgans, the house went through a series of owners.
Courtesy of Bob Romeo, Lenox.

Today, known as Ventfort Hall, the mansion houses the Museum of the Gilded Age, which depicts changes in lifestyle, industry, and society during the nineteenth century.

The Mount was the home of Pulitzer-prize winning author Edith Wharton, who is best known for her novels and short stories. Demonstrating a return to classical simplicity in home design, the house is based on the principles that she outlined in her influential book, *The Decoration of Houses* (1897). Three acres of formal gardens surround the house.

William Douglas Sloane and his brother John ran the W & J Sloane furniture store, which their father had begun in New York City. Mr. and Mrs. William Douglas Sloane built Elm Court in the late nineteenth century. Designed by Peabody and Stearns, the 106-room, Shingle-style mansion required dozens of servants. In 1919, the "Elm Court Talks," held at Elm Court, led to the creation of The League of Nations and The Treaty of Versailles. (Note: the postcard appears to have the wrong name for the house.)

Cranwell has seen several houses on its site. In 1853, Reverend Henry Ward Beecher, who was active in the women's suffrage and the anti-slavery movements, bought the property known as Blossom Hill. He had great hopes, but his affair with a married woman ended his dream. Subsequently, General John Rathbone purchased the property and built the first Wyndhurst. In 1892, John Sloane, co-owner of W & J Sloane, purchased the property, demolished the first Wyndhurst, and built another mansion designed by Peabody and Stearns. Sited on 250 Olmstead-landscaped acres, the estate included stables and farm buildings where Jersey cows were housed. In 1897, Mr. and Mrs. Sloane entertained President and Mrs. William McKinley. Naturally, they made great efforts to impress their guest of honor going so far as to have a fireworks display. Mrs. McKinley was so surprised that she fainted away when the fireworks began.
Courtesy of Bob Romeo, Lenox.

In 1939, the mansion became the Cranwell School run by the Society of Jesus of New England. St. Joseph's Hall is Beecher Cottage at the Cranwell resort today.
Courtesy of Bob Romeo, Lenox.

After the school closed in 1975, it became a premier four-season resort with a championship golf course.
Courtesy of Cranwell Resort, Spa and Golf Club, Lenox, Massachusetts.

In 1893, Anson Phelps Stokes, a merchant, banker, clock manufacturer, and real estate investor, built the one hundred-room Shadowbrook with a 410-foot facade overlooking Stockbridge Bowl. Landscape architect Frederick Law Olmsted designed its grounds. Five years later, Stokes lost a leg as a result of a riding accident and left the 738-acre site.

After several owners, the estate was sold to Andrew Carnegie in 1917. When he died in 1922, his wife sold the estate to the New England Province of the Society of Jesus for use as a Jesuit novitiate.

After a fire destroyed the mansion in March 1956, the Jesuits rebuilt it, but eventually the novitiate closed its doors in 1970.

In 1983, the building was reopened as the Kripalu Center for Yoga & Health, a holistic health center. Its size is still amazing: the Kripalu owners are said to have cleaned and repaired 694 windows, installed two acres of carpet, and painted seven acres of walls!
Courtesy of the Kripalu Center for Yoga & Health.

Henry H. Cook, railroad and real estate tycoon, presented Wheatleigh, an 1893 Italianate mansion, to his daughter, Georgie, as a wedding gift when she married Count Carlos de Heredia. Designed by Peabody and Stearns, the building's entrance hall cuts straight through the width of the house to a wide piazza that views the mountains in the distance and the Olmstead gardens close at hand. Today, this former cottage with its Tiffany windows houses a Berkshire country house hotel.

Hotels, Inns, and Clubs

Of course, not everyone had a lovely cottage — and certainly not all homes could sleep all those many summer visitors. Many stayed at inns or hotels.

By the Gilded Age, the Berkshire Coffee House had become the Curtis Hotel and the center of life in Lenox. The popular actress Fanny Kemble Butler called it "The Old Red Inn."
Courtesy of Bob Romeo, Lenox.

Fanny Kemble Butler made sure that the Curtis Hotel was filled with the best and most interesting people. The hotel, which has been the stopping place for men of note for generations, offered sixty-eight fireplaces, balconies in almost every room, and many mountain views. Guests could enjoy the billiard or card rooms in addition to the tennis courts. Today, it is senior citizen housing.

In 1902, General Thomas Hubbard built the Aspinwall Hotel on the old Aspinwall Woolsey estate for $410,000. The hotel flourished as a popular resort for the financial and political leaders of the day. It had every convenience: steam heat and fireplaces in each room, a telegraph office, its own orchestra, walking and bridle paths, and a carriage and uniformed attendant to meet all trains. Although the Aspinwall heavily advertised its fire prevention capability, it burned to the ground in 1931. Eventually, the Town of Lenox obtained the site and renamed it in honor of John D. Kennedy. Today, it offers excellent cross-country skiing and beautiful views. No motorized vehicles are allowed.
Courtesy of Bob Romeo, Lenox.

The Village Inn was built in 1771. It has been catering to vacation and business travelers for more than two hundred years.
Courtesy of Bob Romeo, Lenox.

John E. Alexandre apparently gave the rental cottage (now Brook Farm Inn) on his property to his butler, James Whittenham. Since the latter had no property, he purchased real estate on Hawthorne Street from Bertia Parsons, the widow of Julius Parsons. In 1949, it became Shadowood Inn. Legend has it that Leonard Bernstein was among the first guests. In the 1970s, Ruth Backes, a direct descendant of Ralph Waldo Emerson, purchased it and changed its name to Brook Farm Inn.
Courtesy of Linda and Phil Halpern, Innkeepers, Brook Farm Inn.

The country counterpart of the city club was the Lenox Club, which offered golf, tennis, and a gathering spot for gentlemen. One stockholder would propose a gentleman; another would "second him."
Courtesy of Bob Romeo, Lenox.

The Lenox Club is still the Lenox Club and is open as "the club" in Lenox for weddings.

Around the turn of the century, Lenox had two rail stations: the New Lenox Station and this Houston Street (Lenoxdale) station.
Courtesy of Bob Romeo, Lenox.

Copyright 1906 by the Rotograph Co.
H 4023 Along the Berkshire Street R R, Berkshire Hills, Mass.
Handcolored.

Old Railroad Arch, 1849
Berkshire Hills, Mass.
B. & A. R. R.

AT THIS POINT THE GRADE IS 82 FEET TO THE MILE.
11935 BETWEEN CHESTER AND HUNTINGTON IN THE BERKSHIRES, MASS.
DETROIT PUBLISHING CO.

A 1767 inn with stone-fenced gardens and a tranquil front porch is the essence of romance in the Berkshires.
Courtesy of Birchwood Inn.

The Berkshire Hills are filled with innumerable lovely walks and drives. Before the advent of the automobile, horses played a major role in life in Lenox; the Hunt, the Show, and the Races were all part of living in Lenox.

The Arts

Income taxes and World War I consigned some Berkshire mansions to the wrecking ball or the careless match, while others were deserted for periods of time or found a different role. Once the Boston Symphony Orchestra made its summer home at Tanglewood, the Berkshires' reputation as a region that combined music, theater, dance, and art with natural beauty began to thrive again.

John Alexandre, a shipping magnate, hired Guy Lowell, the architect of Boston's Museum of Fine Arts, to design Spring Lawn. The first residence designed by Lowell, it blends Beaux-Arts and Classical Revival styles.

Shakespeare & Company

Spring Lawn Mansion went from a private residence to other uses, including a boys' school. In 1999, it became a residence and theater for Shakespeare & Company, founded in 1978. The sixty-three-acre property included the Spring Lawn mansion along with twenty-one other buildings, but many of the buildings were condemned. As it grows, the company is refurbishing some. The main stage theatre, the 428-seat Founders' Theatre, is in the boys' gymnasium. Another building, which was the hockey rink, is now the production center.

Home of one of the larger Shakespeare festivals in the country, Shakespeare & Company also offers one of the most unique and extensive actor training programs by a regional theater in the nation. Theater professionals from all over the world come to train with the company.
Courtesy of Bob Romeo, Lenox.

Tanglewood

In August 1934, members of the New York Philharmonic, directed by Henry Hadley, gave three outdoor concerts at Interlaken. The music-loving residents who had initiated this venture were so pleased that they incorporated the Berkshire Symphonic Festival and repeated the experiment during the next summer.

In the winter of 1936, Mrs. Gorham Brooks and Miss Mary Aspinwall Tappan gave the Tappan family estate, Tanglewood, with its buildings and 210 acres of lawns and meadows to the Boston Symphony Orchestra.

The following year, they invited Serge Koussevitzky and the Boston Symphony Orchestra to participate. On August 13, 1936, the Boston Symphony Orchestra gave three concerts under a large tent at Holmwood, a former Vanderbilt estate, later the Center at Foxhollow. Almost 15,000 people attended.

On August 5, 1937, the festival's largest crowd so far assembled under a tent for the first Tanglewood concert, an all-Beethoven program. In his white tie and tailcoat, Conductor Koussevitzky began the concert with Beethoven's Leonora Overture No. 3.
Courtesy of Birchwood Inn.

By 1940, the Berkshire Music Center (now the Tanglewood Music Center) began its operations. Note how the hairstyles and clothes change.

Today, Tanglewood is the summer home of the Boston Symphony Orchestra. Thousands of music lovers converge on it during June, July, and August to enjoy not only the music but also the extraordinary views of the rolling countryside.
Courtesy of Knut Wefald.

Audience members pack wonderful picnics and lie on the grass and dream in the sun. Some even bring candlesticks! Courtesy of Knut Wefald.

Tanglewood is a sensory delight. Courtesy of Knut Wefald.

Chapter Five:
Pittsfield

In reality, the Berkshire Mountains are two small mountain ranges, the Hoosac Range to the east and the Taconic Range to the west, which separate the region from the surrounding area. These geographic boundaries along with the threats of Indian raids stemming from the French and Indian War led to the area not being settled until 1752.

Originally incorporated as Pontoosuck Plantation, Pittsfield was named after William Pitt, the British nobleman and politician. Initially, the town focused on agriculture, but soon, because of the many brooks that flowed into the Housatonic River, many mills were producing lumber, grist, paper, and textiles. Once Spain's Merino sheep were introduced in 1807, the area became the center of woolen manufacturing in the United States, an industry that would dominate the community's employment opportunities for almost a century.

Pittsfield's streets were wide and lined with trees.

The four principal streets of the town, named from the points of the compass, meet at the park. North Street contains the bulk of the stores and business places.

The county seat, Pittsfield is the largest city in Berkshire County, although the population has declined in recent decades. In 2006, *Forbes* ranked Pittsfield as #61 in its list of "Best Small Places for Business."

In 1868, the court moved from Lenox to Pittsfield.

Art and Culture

The founding of a library in the early nineteenth century was very different than it is today. Initially, the Pittsfield library had no building of its own, and its members passed books around. In the 1830s, a Pittsfield Athenaeum Club was established. Today, it has a Herman Melville Memorial Room and a collection of New England genealogical records and historical materials.

It also has what is believed to be the earliest written reference to baseball in North America in a 1791 Pittsfield bylaw, which states that:

> *...for the Preservation of the Windows in the New Meeting House . . . no Person or Inhabitant of said town, shall be permitted to play at any game called Wicket, Cricket, Baseball, Football, Cat, Fives or any other game or games with balls, within the Distance of Eighty Yards from said Meeting House.*

In 1903, Berkshire Museum founder, Zenas Crane, third generation owner of Crane & Company, wanted to create a new museum for the people of western Massachusetts.

He procured art, collected natural history and science artifacts, and found objects associated with lives of well-known Americans. The result is an eclectic, multipurpose museum primarily mandated to provide education in the arts and sciences.

A collection of Hudson River School landscapes and artifacts is among its art collection.

Schools and Medical Facilities

Briggs School, Pittsfield, Mass.

Miss Halls School, Pittsfield, Mass.

Bishop Memorial Training School for Nurses,
Pittsfield, Mass.

Park Square, Pittsfield, Mass.
205,339

Home for Aged Women,
Pittsfield, Mass.

House of Mercy Hospital, Pittsfield, Mass.
205,391

Industry

In 1804, the textile industry was established in Pittsfield.

The Housatonic River was used to run the power looms, and many worsted and knitting mills were built. In fact, some say that President Madison's inaugural suit was woven here!

During the late nineteenth and early twentieth century, immigrants came to Pittsfield in search of factory jobs, thus creating the diverse ethnic communities found throughout the area.

Pittsfield's population had grown to more than 50,000 by 1930. GE Advanced Materials (Plastics) has continued to be one of the city's largest employers.

Parks and Recreation

Recreation has always been important in the Berkshires. On May 18, 1902, the street railway opened Berkshire Park. A short distance north of the Pittsfield boundary, it offered burro rides, vaudeville acts, balloon ascensions, baseball, theater, and fireworks on its 110 acres. A favorite resort for Pittsfield area residents, it had twenty extra trolleys running on weekends.

Gradually, the trolley lines were discontinued. As late as 1923, Crane and Company employees held an outing at Berkshire Park, but most of them came to the resort by automobile instead of trolley. By 1933, the last of the trolley cars were dismantled. Supposedly, the salvaged steel was used for the Golden Gate Bridge cables!

PITTSFIELD, Mass.
Soldier's
Monument
and Park.

WAR MEMORIAL, PITTSFIELD, MASS. 86
5932-29

Springside Park Lake, Pittsfield, Mass.

The Thomas Allen Memorial in the Pittsfield Cemetery is a forty-two-foot obelisk of polished red marble quarried in Missouri and erected in 1885 on a hill in the High Grove section of the cemetery. Just before it was to be shipped from Missouri, six feet broke off the stone. Even reduced, it's considered the largest piece of polished red marble in the world.

Churches

A 1773 Colonial mansion, the Rectory of St. Stephen's was left to the parish on the condition that only "gentlefolk" should inhabit it.

Thomas Allen of Northampton, a 20-year-old graduate of Harvard College, became the first minister of the meetinghouse in 1764. He is remembered as the "Fighting Parson" who, during the Revolutionary War, carried a musket into his pulpit and fired the first shot against the British at the Battle of Bennington.

The first Methodist sermon was preached in Pittsfield about 1789. By 1791, the Methodist Society in Pittsfield was organized as part of the Stockbridge Circuit. The cornerstone of this building was laid in 1873.

Famous Citizens

On the site of the First Church stood the meetinghouse of "Fighting" Parson Allen, who led the men of the Berkshires to the Battle of Bennington. The Village held a reception for General Lafayette on the Green. Pittsfield is known as a baseball town. Many baseball players came from the city, and Wahconah Park, where baseball has been played since 1892, has attracted baseball fans for generations.

American painters, poets, and authors have been attracted to the Berkshires. Henry Wadsworth Longfellow won the "heart and hand" of Fanny Appleton while she was living in Pittsfield one summer. After their marriage in 1843 in Boston, they took various wedding journeys, including one back to Pittsfield. In the Appleton summer home on East Street, Pittsfield, Longfellow spotted a tall, old-fashioned clock at the top of the stairway. There, he wrote the poem, "The Clock at the Top of the Stairs."

Oliver Wendell Holmes, Boston physician and man of letters, and his son Oliver Wendell Holmes Jr. who served on the United States Supreme Court for thirty years, lived in a fifteen-room cottage known as Holmesdale. Today, it has an in-ground solar-heated pool, enclosed solarium, awning-covered patio, and a gazebo overlooking the tennis court, an in-law cottage, five working fireplaces, and seven bathrooms.

Holmes Senior built the house in 1848 on 280 acres bordered by the Housatonic River. According to his notes, he also planted seven hundred trees.

General William F. Bartlett of Pittsfield fought in the Civil War. He lived in Wendell Hall, and his statue by Daniel Chester French stands in the Memorial Hall of the Massachusetts State House in Boston.

Hotels

By the late nineteenth century, the town became incorporated as a city. The July 11, 1915, issue of the *New York Times* commented, "...both Pittsfield, the commercial and industrial centre (sic) of the region, and Lenox (which is ten miles south) are well provided with excellent hotels and modern garages."

Originally built in 1829 as a school for young men, it became a school for girls. Since 1891, it has been a hotel.

EXTERIOR SOLARIUM, HOTEL WENDELL, PITTSFIELD, MASS.

Maplewood Hotel, Pittsfield, Mass.
Pub. by P. F. McLaughlin.

Country Club, Pittsfield, Mass.
P-68385

Nature

South Mountain is a lovely area in Pittsfield. In the early fall, South Mountain Concerts present chamber music concerts each year.

Lake Mahkeenac, also known as the Stockbridge Bowl, is the site of a town beach, a boating club, and a summer camp. Many cottages ring the lake; during spring and fall, water birds stop here on their migration. From his rented red farmhouse on Stockbridge Bowl, Hawthorne first wrote about the beauty of the land. Eighteen months later he complained that its beauty kept him from his writing!

How The Lake Got Its Name

On a still moonless night in the area near Pittsfield, you may hear the plaintive cry "Shoon-keek" across the quiet Pontoosuc Lake and the response "Moon-keek" echo back from the silent surrounding hill.

Three hundred years before the Europeans came to the region, two brothers settled around the lake now known as Pontoosuc. One brother had a daughter named Moon-keek. The other had a son called Shoon-keek. The two children grew up together, playing in the forests, scrambling under the tangle of grapevines, alders, and red dogwood to find their special hiding spots. Shoon-keek's keen eyes would find a trail marked with deer hooves leading to higher land, and they would climb to the high cliffs. They would lie on the mossy forest carpet under groves of beeches alive with squirrels and bird song. They would watch the beavers build their lodges and the squirrels hide their acorns. They would swim in the beautiful lake, canoe around its edge, and fish in the crystal clear streams.

And as in all stories such as this, he grew strong, and she grew beautiful. Now, the law of all Indian tribes forbids cousins from marrying, and these two were first cousins. Moreover, another brave, Nockawando, wanted to marry Moon-keek. She resisted his overtures, so he went to her father, saying that Moon-keek was too familiar with Shoon-keek and that they were disobeying the tribal customs. He argued that first cousins should not be permitted to be together.

Her father agreed and went to his brother. Together, they agreed that Moon-keek and Shoon-keek had to be separated. This relationship could not continue. Like many young couples, this young couple resisted their parents' attempt to part them. They would sneak out and meet whenever they could. They met on the mountaintops, in the forests, and in the valleys. They used their birchbark canoes for transportation, finding secluded spots and islands on the perimeter of the lake. Every day they met, and every day they were a little bolder with each other. Finally, they decided to leave the area and ask another tribe to adopt them. They planned to meet at one of their favorite islands. They promised to meet beneath the lake, if anything interfered with their flight.

The night that they planned to leave, the jealous Nockawando was spying on Moon-keek, afraid that she would leave the tribe. He watched her leave her father's lodge and silently walk to her canoe and paddle to a distant island. He then went to Shoon-keek's lodge and watched him quietly leave his father's lodge and board his canoe. Nockawando got into his canoe and paddled softly after Shoon-keek. When Nockawando was within range, he shot Shoon-keek with an arrow. The young lover fell into the dark lake waters.

But his canoe continued on and on—as if paddled by an invisible spirit. When it swiftly passed the island where Moon-keek waited, she had a premonition about the events that had occurred. She leapt into her own canoe and pushed out from shore. Nockawando heard her raise her death-song and paddled as rapidly as he could, but near the middle of the lake his arm stopped paddling as if gripped by a stronger force than he.

The night became strangely still. There wasn't even the sound of the loon or a rustle of a leaf. He watched as she called, "Shoon-keek, Shoon-keek." The lake answered, "Moon-keek. Moon-keek." As Nockawando watched, Moon-keek slipped into the lake, and the waters closed gently over her head. Her canoe glided on to join Shoon-keek's empty canoe. The next day, they Indians looked for their bodies, but they were never found. The Indians believe, however, that they were together, paddling their birchbark canoes. On the nights when the moon rises from the water, the Indians often see the two canoes skimming the waters of the lake on dark nights, sometimes together, sometimes a little apart — but not very far. Sometimes they hear the cry "Moon-keek" and the answer "Shoon-keek." And so they named the lake after these two who would not be parted.

Constitution Hill, which overlooks Pontoosuc Lake, was the home of Jonathan Smith. His speech aided in bringing about the ratification of the Constitution by the Massachusetts Convention in 1788:

> *I am a plain man, and get my living by the plough... I have lived in a part of the country where I have known the worth of good government by the want of it.*

The Frog Rock or "Frog's Landing" is an approximately twenty-five-ton stone that looks like an enormous sitting frog gazing south down the narrow river. Supposedly, it was painted to resemble a frog, and postcards were printed up. During the rebuilding of the old waterfall, the frog was put on a concrete pad to preserve it.

The jewel of the Berkshires is often said to be Pontoosuc Lake in Pittsfield. Also known as Moonkeek, the 480-acre Pontoosuc Lake has many summer cottages around its shore. In the park separating it from Onota Lake is a great boulder that was split by a birch tree growing through it. It is known simply as Split Rock!

Nearby is Balance Rock, a pyramidal limestone boulder of 165 tons delicately balanced on a little rock. Many have tried to push it off, but it still stands. From this park can be seen the northern Berkshires and Taconics, with Constitution Hill in the foreground. Against the northern horizon is Mount Greylock, sixteen miles away. The area is the subject of many legends.

PONTOOSUC LAKE, PITTSFIELD, MASS. 146P
5A-H2032

Pontoosuc Lake, Pittsfield, Mass. in the Berkshires—160
1B-H1946

Honasada Pavilion, Pontoosuc Lake, Pittsfield Mass.

BOAT CLUB AND AUDITORIUM, PONTOOSUC LAKE, PITTSFIELD, MASS. 78

The White Deer of Onata

By the early seventeenth century, the French were encroaching on the British territory in America. Already, France claimed most of North America west of the Appalachian Mountains. Jacques Cartier (1542) and Samuel de Champlain (1608) had established military outposts along the St. Lawrence River and into the Great Lakes, founding the territory known as New France. Trappers, traders, and Jesuit missionaries along with Indians inhabited this wilderness.

They competed for the Indians' furs and control of the native tribes and searched for the path to the Pacific. They learned the Indian dialects and adopted their habits while trying to convert them to Christianity.

Because of the riches to be found in the New World, many young French nobles sailed to New France to find their fortune. To get ahead in the French Court, you had to please the king: Louis XV. All the courtiers knew that he loved presents: jewels, gold, and furs.

During the early days of the French and Indian War, an ambitious French officer named Montalbert was sent to Berkshire County to persuade the Housatonic Indians to wage war against the English. Unlike the English who took axes and saws to the wilderness, the French were adventurers — not settlers. Montalbert was not just a mere adventurer; he was an ambitious man. He wanted to climb the ranks of nobility.

The Housatonic Indians were a prosperous tribe living near to the deep, spring-fed Lake Onoto, which supplied them with fish and game. They attributed their good fortune to a white doe, which came to drink from the lake. Obviously, she was a good omen. One of their prophets had predicted, "So long as the white doe drinks at Onota, pestilence, famine, and foe would never lay waste to their land."

The Housatonic Indians threatened anyone who tried to harm their white doe with swift retribution. They treated the doe so well that she allowed them to touch her, to pat her, and even to play with her.

When Montalbert visited the village, he learned of the white doe. "What a treasure that would be!" he thought. "Such a unique curiosity! If it could bring happiness and prosperity to a small band of heathens, think what it could do for King Louis XV! And most certainly the king would reward his Montalbert accordingly. My fortune would be made, if I just brought the king the doe's skin."

The enterprising Montalbert immediately offered a great reward to the hunter who brought him the skin of the white deer. The Indians were appalled. The doe was sacred. Anyone who harmed it would quickly feel their vengeance. Recognizing this, Montalbert decided to find another way to obtain the doe.

In his meetings with the tribe, he noticed that one Indian named Wondo loved rum. He would do almost anything for a drink, and Montalbert, like other ambitious white men, had brought lots of rum for bribing susceptible Indians. Realizing that Wondo was the weak link, Montalbert plied him with rum.

Once Wondo had succumbed to the bribe of rum and no longer adhered to his tribe's values, Montalbert said he would give him a bottle of rum in exchange for the white doe. Rum was the most important thing in the world to Wondo — certainly more important than a white doe. So he brought the white doe to him. The doe came eagerly because she trusted people — even a drunken Indian didn't bother her. The Indians had always brought her joy and happiness, but the ambitious Montalbert wasn't an Indian, and he killed the white doe with one quick blow. Placing her blood-splashed skin in his saddlebag, he left quickly for Canada.

Once Wondo finished his bottle of rum and realized that he had been manipulated, he felt awful. Not being able to live with his guilt, he confessed to his crime, and the tribe dealt with him swiftly. Then the tribe set out to stop Montalbert, hoping that they could prevent the approaching disaster.

The storytellers say that Montalbert never reached Canada, and Louis XV never received the skin of the white deer. But the prosperity of the Indian tribe was no more. Wars, disease, and emigration followed. In a few years, not a wigwam was left standing besides Onoto.

Honasada Pavilion, Pontoosuc Lake, Pittsfielu Mass.

Scene in Beautiful Burbank Park, Onota Lake, Pittsfield, Mass. — D-35

Causeway across Onota Lake, Pittsfield, Mass.

Scene on Onoto Lake, Pittsfield, Mass.

View of Onota Lake,
Pittsfield, Mass.

152—Bathing Beach, Onota Lake,
9A-H1946

The Hancock Shaker Village

The United Society of Believers in Christ's Second Appearing was founded in England in 1747. The sect is more commonly known as the Shakers because of their frenzied religious dancing. Their beliefs emphasize community, sexual equality, spiritual contemplation, pacifism, and a personal relationship with God. In 1774, the Shakers emigrated to the United States; the Hancock community was founded in 1790.
Courtesy of Hancock Shaker Village, Pittsfield, Massachusetts.

The Hancock Shaker Village in Pittsfield, Massachusetts, is a popular tourist attraction. Visitors have the unique opportunity of dropping back in time by a century or two and touring this graceful renovated village with its twelve hundred acres of farm, woodland, and pasture. Heritage breeds of animals such as shorthorn cattle, Merino sheep and silver-laced Wyandotte and Dominique chickens roam the fields. Two heirloom vegetable gardens contain plant varieties on Shaker seed lists from the 1830s and 1890s, respectively.
Courtesy of Hancock Shaker Village, Pittsfield, Massachusetts.

Known as "The City of Peace," the village contains the largest and most representative collection of Shaker artifacts available to the public at an original Shaker site.
Courtesy of Hancock Shaker Village, Pittsfield, Massachusetts.

The buildings hold a major collection of Shaker furniture and household items. Today, Shaker furniture is prized for its simple elegance.
Courtesy of Hancock Shaker Village, Pittsfield, Massachusetts.

The Round Stone Barn is an architectural gem. Built in 1825, the barn was widely cited during the 1880s as "machinelike in its efficiency" and "a model for the soundest dairying practices." Settlers on the Great Plains dotted the frontier with timber versions of it—most of which have now disappeared.
Courtesy of Hancock Shaker Village, Pittsfield, Massachusetts.

Well known for their medicinal herb and garden seed industries, Shaker communities cultivated herbs, raised produce for seed, and processed herbs and plants (e.g., belladonna, hops, native ginger, chicory, black cohosh, basil, poppies, and pennyroyal) for sale to the "World." Supposedly, seed packets began with them!
Courtesy of D. Peter Lund.

A private, not-for-profit educational organization, the village was opened in 1961 and designated a National Historic Landmark in 1968. Its mission is to bring the Shaker story to life and preserve it for future generations.
Courtesy of Hancock Shaker Village, Pittsfield, Massachusetts.

Chapter Six:
Dalton

Dalton was settled in 1755. Although its residents were farmers, Dalton is famous for its mills along the East Branch of the Housatonic River, which flows through the valley.

In 1879, Crane began producing the rag-based paper used for U.S. currency. Since that time, it has produced that paper, along with formal stationary used by heads of state to prospective brides!
Courtesy of Crane & Co., Inc.

In 1801, Zenas Crane established a paper mill. By 1806, local and regional banks began printing currency on Crane's cotton papers, which was quickly followed by official government proclamations, permanent public records, and stocks and bonds.
Courtesy of Crane & Co., Inc.

First opened in the autumn of 1930, the Crane Museum of Papermaking is on the National Register of Historic Places. The one-story building is situated on the banks of the Housatonic River, which supplied the water to wash the rags and drive the machinery of the early Crane mills. Courtesy of Crane & Co., Inc.

Between Dalton and Windsor are the Waconah Falls, dropping eighty feet over a gray marble cliff. These waterfalls are the subject of several Native American legends.

The river is the source of several brooks and waterfalls.

Wahconah of Wahconah Falls

Wahconah Falls flows over several smaller tiered falls and then cascades into a deep pool. People who know how to listen to waterfalls say that sometimes these falls murmur happily because the wicked have been outwitted. At other times, they roar with laughter.

Chief Miacomo had ruled it for forty years when Yonnongah, an aging Mohawk warlord, came to woo his beautiful daughter Wahconah. Yonnongah had three wives already, but he was determined to add Wahconah to his collection.

One June day, the girl sat beside the cascade named for her, braiding flowers in her hair and watching leaves float down the stream. Suddenly, she sensed that someone was watching her. She leapt to her feet in alarm as Nessacus, a handsome young brave, stepped forward, exclaiming, "Hail, Bright Star!"

"Hail, brother," answered Wahconah.

"I am Nessacus," said the man, "One of King Philip's soldiers. My people and I are tired from our flight from the Long Knives (the English). Can we rest in your village? "

The maiden answered, "My father is away, in council with the Mohawks, but his wigwams are always open. Please come with me."

Nessacus signaled to his tired, battle-worn troops. Wahconah led them down to her valley, where they were welcomed. As Nessacus' people were getting acquainted with Wahconah's tribe, the two young people found much to occupy their time. During the next several weeks, they wandered the fields carpeted in the green and gold of fresh grass, walked along the upper portion of the falls, and swam under the gurgling waterfall. Soon, they were very much in love.

When her father Miacomo returned, he brought with him the elderly Mohawk suitor and the scheming priest, Tashmu, whom no one liked. During the next several weeks, the tribe and its visitors played many games of skill and strength and had several great feasts. The youthful Nessacus easily won the games of skill, while the battle-scarred warrior Yonnongah won the games of strength. The young lovers wanted to be together, but they had to obtain permission first. Nessacus quietly studied his opponent the way he analyzed his hunting grounds. He knew that to succeed in obtaining Wahconah's hand, he had to understand the environment in which his opponent lived, the values that he had, and the methods that he used.

When Nessacus asked Wahconah's father permission to marry his daughter, Chief Miacomo was most pleased. He was ready to announce their engagement when Tashmu, the devious priest, intervened, advising him to give the girl to Yonnongah. A friendship with Yonnongah's tribe might be beneficial, given the expansion of the English, he said. Such a marriage would cement the bonds between the tribes.

The situation was at impasse until Nessacus suggested that Yonnongah and he hold a duel; the winner would marry Wahconah. Yonnongah accepted his challenge, but the crafty Tashmu pointed to the negative omens in the voices of wind and thunder, the flight of the birds, and the shape of the clouds. No good would come of such a duel, he warned. There would be problems. The Chief should let the Great Spirit and his wise priest Tashmu decide instead.

"Go," snapped Chief Miacomo. "Commune with the wind and stars at Wizard's Glen. Let them tell us what to do."

Tashmu forbade anyone to leave the Indian village while he conferred with the wind and the stars. When it was dark, he went to the pool below the falls. Midway on the downstream side of the pool, he laid a great rock, dividing the current just about evenly. Working late into the night, he submerged many large rocks in the stream on one side, which diverted a greater share of water into the other.

In the morning, Tashmu announced that the Great Spirit had decreed that a canoe should be floated into the middle of the pool and left to drift. If it passed downstream on one side of the big rock, Nessacus was to have the girl. If it went to the other side, the great warrior Yonnongah would win. The assembled tribe listened eagerly for they wanted the lovely Wahconah to marry the young Nessacus.

Everyone gathered on the shores of the stream: Nessacus was on one side and Yonnongah on another. Tashmu set free the canoe; slowly, very slowly, it drifted toward the great stone. As it approached, it gained speed, veering one way and then the other. A shifting wind turned it sideways, and it struck the dividing rock amidships. The tribe groaned. Then the current swung it around, a gust of wind caught it, and it swept past Nessacus — the winner! The tribe cheered their approval.

"The Great Spirit has spoken, and it is good," said Chief Miacomo. Dismayed, Tashmu and Yonnongah disappeared soon afterward, but not before Tashmu discovered that all the big rocks he had so carefully sunk on Nessacus' side of the brook weren't there. Someone had tricked him, and he knew who it was!

As the wedding festivities were progressing, a messenger brought word that the Long Knives were planning to destroy Chief Miacomo's tribe. Nessacus took Wahconah by the hand, promising to lead the tribe and her to a new home via the western trail.

Chapter Seven:
Jacob's Ladder Region

Jacob's Ladder Scenic Byway and the Westfield River wind through the small towns of Russell, Huntington, Chester, Becket, and Lee. This Berkshire region is quietly beautiful with village greens, white water for canoeing or kayaking, handcrafted keystone bridges, and local artisans.

Jacob's Ladder Scenic Byway or the "Jacob's Ladder Trail" is a thirty-three-mile state highway, beginning at Lee's picturesque village green and continuing on Route 20 to the Westfield border. Originally a footpath traveled by Native Americans, Jacob's Ladder Trail was a main route between the Connecticut and Hudson River valleys.

The Massachusetts Turnpike looking west, nine miles east of the Lee Interchange.
Courtesy of Geoffrey H. Goldberg.

Jacob's Ladder Trail ascends to its highest elevation at Morey Hill, in the town of Becket.

A stone cairn originally placed there for the gala inauguration of the highway in September 1910 marks the summit. In the early part of the twentieth century, cars often become overheated climbing the hills. Motorists would stop here to refill their radiators at Jacob's Well and Spring.

The cairn and the former summit house are all that is left of what was once a popular destination in its heyday.

In 1910, the road, which was billed as "the First of the Great Mountain Crossovers," was opened as the first highway built specifically for the new horseless carriages. Motorists from all over came to test themselves and their machines against the rugged terrain. Several years later, the trail became part of the highway called "Yellowstone Trail," which linked Massachusetts to Oregon.

The name "Jacob's Ladder Trail" is steeped in legend. One story says that it was named after the biblical Jacob, while others attribute the name to Jacob Carter, a member of the family who found a large-pillow-shaped rock on their property, which they named Jacob's Pillow. Another legend says that the original trail had many water bars to prevent washouts. An ambitious local farmer named Jacob would flood the water bars so that horse-drawn carriages and later automobiles would get stuck in the mud holes. An enterprising man, Jacob would then approach the unfortunate driver and suggest that the driver could hire him and his team of oxen to tow the stranded vehicle out of the mire!

Lee is often called "The Gateway to the Berkshires." Built around its marble quarry and paper mills, Lee has what is called a traditional New England main street, but today it also offers a large shopping mall.

The earliest settler in Becket established a sawmill on Walker Brook in the eastern part of the town in 1751. Incorporated in 1765, the town also developed such industries as charcoal, ash basketry, granite, raw silk processing, and dairying, but after the 1927 flood, most of the industries died out.

Today, Jacob's Pillow, a National Historic Landmark, has made Becket famous. As a home for dance in the United States, it encompasses an internationally acclaimed summer dance festival (the longest running in the United States), a professional school, rare and extensive archives, an intern program, and year-round community programs on the site of Becket's historic (c. 1790) Carter Farm.

During the course of the ten-week festival, companies from around the world present 150 performances on three stages. Dance styles include contemporary, modern, ballet, dance-theatre, jazz, tap, hip-hop, and ethnic.
Courtesy of Jacob's Pillow Dance.

More than two hundred free events – open rehearsals, outdoor performances, open studios, daily talks by scholars-in-residence, exhibits, film and video showings, and panel discussions – are available to the public.
Courtesy of Jacob's Pillow Dance.

Chapter Eight:
Rowe

A small hill town in northwestern Massachusetts, Rowe is nestled in an area of scenic beauty, with wooded mountains, clear brooks and the Deerfield River on its border. Visitors to Rowe enjoy great skiing, hiking, fishing, hunting, canoeing, and kayaking.

Rowe grew around the mills on the river, but it also had sulfur, talc, and soapstone mining industries. In the late 1880s, with the addition of the railroad along the river, it became a small resort town for a period of time. This gazebo is in the center of town.
Courtesy of Maple House.

Colonists came to Rowe in 1744; the area was the site of a fort to guard against raids. In 1762, Reverend Cornelius Jones purchased the town lands, calling it "Myrifield" after the Greek word for "thousand." By 1785, the Massachusetts General Court incorporated it as a town, renaming it for John Rowe, a prominent Boston merchant.
Courtesy of Maple House.

In 1960, Rowe became the site of the Yankee Rowe Nuclear Power Station, New England's first nuclear power plant. In 1992, the plant was decommissioned. This Stone Church was built around 1780.
Courtesy of Maple House.

Maple House Bed and Breakfast is a two hundred-year-old inn that is still in business.
Courtesy of Maple House.

Chapter Nine:

Mohawk Trail & its Environs

The Mohawk trail, often displayed on maps as Massachusetts Route 2, runs from Millers Falls on the Connecticut River to the Massachusetts-New York border. Initially, the trail was a Native American footpath. The Mohawks used it in their raids on the Connecticut Valley settlements; the pioneers used it; and later Benedict Arnold led an army down it.

In 1914, as the automobile became popular, the Massachusetts Legislature declared the Mohawk Trail to be the first scenic route in the Commonwealth. After all, it offers glorious sunrises and golden sunsets, purple hills, and deep gorges with hidden falls, cascades, and tumbling streams. As the July 11, 1915, issue of the *New York Times* said, "Not only is the scenery delightful, but historic spots abound in the hill towns." Subsequently, the *National Geographic Traveler* selected the Mohawk Trail as one of fifty such scenic routes in the United States. The American Automobile Association also chose "The Trail" with its deserted Indian trails, craggy slopes, and wonderful wildlife for scenic recognition, as has the federal government in one of its national programs.

Courtesy of Geoffrey Goldberg.

Turners Falls is the cutlery center of New England. To aid in the navigation of the river, a dam and canal were built in 1792. In 1866, the Turners Falls Company built a curved dam, 1000 feet long. The sandstone along the riverbed is famous for fossil reptilian foot tracks, popularly known as "bird tracks."
Courtesy of Geoffrey Goldberg.

Miller's Falls began to develop as a manufacturing center in 1869. The route crosses the river and runs high above the deep gorge.
Courtesy of Geoffrey Goldberg.

The French King Bridge was part of a Massachusetts Highway project to relocate a particularly hazardous seven-mile stretch of the old Mohawk Trail Highway (State Route 2) between Erving and Greenfield in 1932. The American Institute of Steel Construction named the French King Bridge the most beautiful steel bridge of its class erected in America in 1932.
Courtesy of Geoffrey H. Goldberg.

In 1992, the bridge was rebuilt to suit the setting of the gorge. The 1992 rehabilitation project won the 1993 Massachusetts Historic Commission Preservation Award.
Courtesy of Geoffrey H. Goldberg.

Birches abound through the Berkshires.
Courtesy of Birchwood Inn.

From the east, the Mohawk Trail begins at the town of Greenfield, located among the green and fertile fields (of course) at the confluence of the Connecticut and Deerfield Rivers.

An agricultural and industrial center, Greenfield is the site of the nation's first cutlery factory.

Greenfield is just north of Deerfield, which was founded in 1663 on the lush river plain. Considered the best preserved colonial village in New England, Deerfield has forty-six buildings erected before 1850 along the mile-long main street. With their antique furnishings, along with the exhibition galleries and collections, these houses and their costumed interpreters comprise some of the finest examples of publicly available Americana in the United States.

The Deerfield Massacre

Deerfield's most infamous story is the 1704 Deerfield Massacre, when French and Indian forces attacked the town a few hours before dawn on a chilly February morning. The invaders came more than three hundred miles, mostly by snowshoe, to kill settlers or take them prisoner, burn houses, and slaughter livestock. Part of the War of the Spanish Succession, this attack was an effort by the French and Indians to halt the English expansion to the northeast.

They struck at dawn, razing Deerfield and killing some fifty colonists, including children. One hundred and nine survivors, including women and children, totaling more than half of the town's residents, were taken captive and force marched on a grueling, three hundred snow-covered mile trek to Quebec.

One captive was Eunice Williams, who was married to Reverend John Williams, the Congregational minister in Deerfield. Like most women of her day, pregnancy, childbirth, and the nursing of infants dominated her life. She had a child almost every other year between her wedding at age 22 and her death at 39.

War cries and war-painted Indians burst through the Williams' door that fatal morning. During those first terrible moments, Eunice looked on helplessly while the Indians threatened to kill her husband. They did kill her six-week old baby, another child, and a female slave. They dragged the rest of the family, including her husband John, out of the house. The long march began.

En route, the Indians killed those who couldn't keep up the pace. Still recovering from childbirth, Eunice Williams was very weak. Knowing her strength was failing, she said goodbye to her husband, wishing that he and at least some of their children would survive. When they crossed a swift-running river in Greenfield, not far from today's Mohawk Trail, Eunice slipped on a rock and plunged into the water. Her body, soaked with water and blood, was left behind. After crossing the Green River and climbing a steep hill, John Williams waited, asking all who passed if they had seen his wife. On hearing of her fate, he was devastated. Later, a search party found Eunice's body and buried her in Deerfield.

Many Deerfield residents died along the way, but the Indians and many colonials, including John Williams, reached Fort Chambly, Quebec, in seven weeks. The French pressured him to convert to Catholicism, but he refused. During the next two years, he remained remarkably optimistic.

In November 1706, the surviving captives were finally set free and returned to Boston. Four of the Williams' children were redeemed and returned to New England, one continuing into the ministry. Upon his return, the Reverend Williams wrote an account of his captivity, *The Redeemed Captive Returning to Zion* (1707), to heighten awareness of the Deerfield raid.

One daughter, Eunice Williams (1696-1786), was seven years old when taken into captivity. She absorbed the lifestyle of her Mohawk family. Despite repeated attempts by her father and English officials to convince her to leave, Eunice refused. Although Indians had killed her mother, she wanted something other in life than living as a wife of a colonist. Every one had an idea about the appropriate happy ending for her, but she knew differently.

At age sixteen in 1713, Eunice married Arosen, a Mohawk. She received the Mohawk name A'ongote, which means "She (was) taken and placed (as a member of their tribe)." They had at least three children, two daughters and a son. Both daughters married Indian men, one of whom became the grand chief of the village; the other was also a prominent figure. The fact that her daughters married so well indicates that Eunice's adopted tribe held her in high esteem.

The assimilation of Deerfield residents into Native American communities has fostered ongoing relationships between Deerfield and several Native American nations. Over the years, formal and informal gatherings and events have celebrated these connections.

The ghost of Eunice's mother, however, is still thought to wander unhappily about the bridge. She lost several children and her own life in the raid and on the march to Canada. Perhaps worst of all was that her namesake abandoned her own family and its colonial values for a life with the very savages who destroyed her family. But mothers often disagree with their children's choices!

A worthwhile side trip, the town's museum offers nineteen exhibit rooms and many concerts throughout the season.

Courtesy of the Pocumtuck Valley Memorial Association, Memorial Hall Museum, Deerfield, Massachusetts.

The Mohawk Trail swings around Greenfield Mountain to enter the deep, steep-walled Deerfield River Valley.

The beautiful Deerfield River is an integral part of Shelburne, located just off the trail.
Courtesy of the Shelburne Historical Society.

Shelburne is dedicated to preserving the simplicity of the past. Its residents express their pride in their restored buildings, spectacular surroundings and New England spirit.
Courtesy of the Shelburne Historical Society.

Once a prime salmon fishing ground, the village became a manufacturing center. Linus Yale made the first Yale locks in Shelburne. The Historical Society houses a museum in the Arms Academy building.
Courtesy of the Shelburne Historical Society.

The towns of Buckland and Shelburne are connected just above Salmon Falls by the famous Bridge of Flowers, an arched trolley bridge. When the trolleys ceased operations, the enterprising Shelburne Falls Women's Club transformed the abandoned bridge into a pedestrian garden bridge, which blooms from spring to fall.
Courtesy of the Shelburne Historical Society.

The glacial potholes are rock formations carved into the riverbed. They are located below the Salmon Falls, which are named for the salmon that used to be found here.
Courtesy of the Shelburne Historical Society.

Courtesy of Geoffrey H. Goldberg.

Courtesy of the Shelburne Historical Society.

The trail traverses the Deerfield River Valley before following the deep gorge of the tributary Cold River to the top of the plateau. This is apple orchard country.

Today, the town has an historic, turn-of-the-century setting and a unique mix of locally owned businesses.
Courtesy of the Shelburne Historical Society.

Zoar Outdoor is based in a 1748 Charlemont homestead, built by Moses Rice, the town's first settler. The nationally recognized whitewater canoe and kayak school provides instruction for beginners to experts. Its rafting program maintains a fleet of eighteen, thirteen-foot self-bailing rafts and nine, thirteen-foot bailer rafts on the Deerfield River.
Courtesy of Zoar Outdoor.

About seven miles from Shelburne Falls, the trail reaches the hilltop town of Charlemont, a small community located along Deerfield River. Settled in 1744, Charlemont offers many recreational opportunities from white-water rafting to trout fishing.

At Mohawk Indian Bridge, the highway reaches Mohawk Park and its landmark "Hail To The Sunrise," a Mohawk Indian Memorial to the Five Indian Nations of the Mohawk Trail. The bronze Mohawk Indian looks to the east with arms uplifted to the Great Spirit. The 900-pound bronze casting is erected on a nine-ton boulder. The Route 2 monument includes inscribed stones from various tribes and councils from throughout the United States.
Courtesy of D. Peter Lund.

The bridge over Deerfield River at Charlemont.
Courtesy of Geoffrey H. Goldberg.

After crossing the Deerfield River Valley, the Mohawk Trail follows the deep gorge of the tributary Cold River to the top of the plateau. Then the highway drops abruptly 1,000 feet to North Adams and the Hoosac River Valley with Mount Greylock towering in the distance.
Courtesy of Geoffrey H. Goldberg.

Further along the road, the Mohawk Trail State Forest has over 6,000 acres of mountain ridges, deep gorges, and tall old-growth trees supporting plant and animal life. With eighteen miles of rivers and streams flowing through it, the Mohawk Forest is famous for its trout fishing.

The BPOE Memorial Elk on Whitcomb Summit is the highest point (2,240 feet) along the Mohawk Trail.

From the summit, you can see into four states, several mountain ranges, rivers, lakes, villages, and cities. In September 1914, 1,800 people gathered here to dedicate the new Mohawk Trail made specifically for automobile excursions through pine-scented forest and pastoral valleys.

Savoy State Forest, with its fifty miles of wooded trails, waterfalls, ponds, and old Indian trails, is located in the Town of Florida. Colonial settlers came to this area to log and farm. Evidence of their industry still exists. Cellar holes, stonewalls, family graveyards, and sawmill sites can be found throughout the forest.

By 1915, cars were becoming more popular. The first scenic route in the nation, the Mohawk Trail offered a great route to try out a new car!
Courtesy of Geoffrey H. Goldberg.

Families took auto excursions and enjoyed the tea-shops, trading posts, and campgrounds on route.
Courtesy of Geoffrey H. Goldberg.

The challenge of driving over the Hoosac Mountain drew families to the Mohawk Trail. Here is the hairpin curve in 1925.
Courtesy of Geoffrey H. Goldberg.

The town of Florida was incorporated in 1805. It's the site of the eastern portal of the Hoosac Tunnel.

43. WHERE THE MOHAWK TRAIL CROSSES THE HOOSAC TUNNEL, BERKSHIRE HILLS, MASS.

UP THE MOUNTAIN FROM HAIRPIN CURVE, MOHAWK TRAIL IN THE BERKSHIRES, MASS.

HAIRPIN CURVE, MOHAWK TRAIL, BERKSHIRE HILLS, MASS.

In the early twentieth century, the train, via the Hoosac Tunnel, was the fastest way from North Adams to Boston.

The Hoosac Tunnel

In the nineteenth century, the Berkshire Mountains, which are intersected by valleys and rivers, separated the region from the rest of the world. In 1819, legislators proposed a canal to transport goods and raw materials between Boston and points West, but the enormity of the project overwhelmed its supporters.

With the advent of the steam locomotive, a tunnel was considered. In 1848, with the slogan "On to Hoosac, on to the West," the Troy and Greenfield line was established, and the tunnel project was a reality. On May 20, 1853, the *New York Daily Times* reported:

> The Hoosac Tunnel, on the scale adopted by the Railroad Company, is a work of stupendous grandeur to contemplate. Its accomplishment will certainly be a proud day for American Railway enterprise. It will be 8,000 yards or nearly five miles in continuous length and in cost and masonry will be scarcely second to the great Leeds and Manchester Tunnel in England.

With the bore initially planned to cost $2,000,000, work began in 1851. Hundreds of miners, using mostly black powder, shovels, picks, and their hands began to bore through Hoosac Mountain. During the summer of 1852, "Wilson's Patented Stone-Cutting Machine" began boring into the east side of the mountain. After excavating about ten feet, the machine died.

Using manpower, hand-drills, and gunpowder meant slow progress. The tunnel construction project required excavation of 2 million tons (1,800,000 metric tons) of rock. Tunnel builders resorted to hand digging and hand drills and later used the Burleigh Rock Drill, one of the first pneumatic drills. The project also saw the first large-scale commercial use of electric blasting caps and nitroglycerin, a new and effective but extremely unstable explosive. Completed in 1875, the tunnel provided more direct rail service to urban centers and to their markets. Originally estimated to cost $2 million, the final cost of the tunnel was more than $14 million plus the lives of two hundred workers.

Many think the ghosts of the almost two hundred men who died constructing the Hoosac Tunnel still lurk in within its dark, clammy interior. People report seeing swaying lanterns and hearing the sound of chisels, as well as the wails of dying men. If you go to the Florida portal, you can meet "ghost hunters!" Some scoff at the ghost stories, but no one likes to be there for long.

Visitors who wish to visit Hoosac Tunnel should be aware of the dangers. About four freight trains go through the tunnel each day: therefore, you don't want to be in the tunnel, looking for orbs and listening for voices. If you're interested in the historical aspects of the tunnel though, you can visit the museum in the Western Gateway Heritage State Park.

Settled in 1737, North Adams was a mill town for most of its existence. When the tunnel was completed, North Adams boomed. Its major industry was textiles.
Courtesy of North Adams Historical Society.

Started in 1851, the Hoosac Tunnel wasn't completed until 1875. An engineering marvel, this 4.7-mile railroad tunnel was the second longest tunnel in the world and the longest tunnel in North America until the 1920s when the Moffat Tunnel was built west of Denver. Listed on the Historic American Engineering Survey and the National Register, the Hoosac Tunnel goes through the Hoosac Range, an extension of Vermont's Green Mountains, to the city of North Adams, in the northwest corner of Massachusetts.
Courtesy of D. Peter Lund.

North Adams also had shoe and hat factories, a brick yard; a saw mill, cabinet-makers, machine shops, marble works, wagon and sleigh-makers, and an ironworks.
Courtesy of North Adams Historical Society.

North Adams is also the site of the Massachusetts Museum of Contemporary Art (MASS MoCA), which fills four large former mill buildings with changing exhibits and performances. This exhibit being installed is entitled "Sunlight In An Empty Room (Passing Cloud for Emily Dickinson, Amherst, Massachusetts, August 28, 2004)."
Courtesy of MASS MoCA.

MASS MoCA is a vehicle for the creation and presentation of contemporary art and develops links to the region's cultural institutions. Its red brick buildings with bridges, viaducts, and elevated walkways lend a distinct architectural ambiance.
Courtesy of MASS MoCA.

Across the wide valley towers Mount Greylock, one of the highest peaks in the Taconic Mountains, a long range that stretches along New York's eastern border from northern Connecticut to central Vermont.

At 3,491 feet, Mount Greylock is the highest point in the purple Berkshire Hills. There you find wild flowers blossoming two to three weeks later than in the valleys below. The snow falls earlier and lingers later. Often clouds and mist obscure the heights when the valley is clear.

Chief Greylock was born around 1660 near what is now the Town of Westfield, Massachusetts. At this time, ownership of territories in northern New England was in flux. The French were established in the north, calling their region New France. The English had settled in the south or New England and along the seaboard. The Indians, who had lived in the region for generations, were largely overlooked, except for their value as allies in war.

Some time in the early nineteenth century, people began to call the mountain Greylock—maybe because of the gray clouds that clouded its peak or maybe to honor Chief Greylock. By the mid-nineteenth century, Mount Greylock had played host to many writers, including Nathaniel Hawthorne, William Cullen Bryant, Oliver Wendell Holmes, Herman Melville, and Henry David Thoreau.

Chief Greylock is said to have lived in a secret cave on the slopes of Mount Greylock, where he harassed the British settlers as they moved into his domain. When war broke out between the French and the British, Greylock and his warriors aligned themselves with the French. While hunting, his foot was crushed in a bear trap. Half his foot had to be amputated, but it never slowed him down.

The highest point in Massachusetts, Mount Greylock became Massachusetts' first state park in 1898.
Courtesy of Birchwood Inn Massachusetts.

The Veterans War Memorial Tower is a perpetually lighted beacon to honor the state's dead from World War I (and subsequent conflicts). The light used to be the strongest beacon in Massachusetts, with a range of seventy miles.

Today, the Massachusetts Department of Conservation and Recreation, Division of State Parks and Recreation, manages the 12,500-acre state reservation with approximately seventy miles of trails, including part of the Appalachian Trail.
Courtesy of D. Peter Lund.

By the late nineteenth century, the mountain had been almost destroyed by clear-cutting logging practices for the local wood, paper, and charcoal industries. A group of concerned local businessmen incorporated the Greylock Park Association (GPA) in 1885, one of the earliest land conservation groups in the state.

The trail is approximately sixty miles, but you can enjoy the gentle mountain scenery and peaceful valleys in all seasons.

The last major town on the Mohawk Trail is Williamstown, the home of Williams College, a town known for walking and biking.

The Sterling & Francine Clark Art Institute, near the college, is a star attraction. The institute offers a large collection of nineteenth century French paintings, including masterpieces by Renoir, Monet and Corot. Its American collection includes Sargent, Cassatt, Remington, and Winslow Homer.

Bibliography

Abbott, Katharine. *Old Paths and Legends of the New England Borders*. New York, New York: G.P. Putnam's Sons, 1907.

Amory, Cleveland. *The Last Resorts*. New York, New York: Harper & Brothers, 1952

Byron, Carl R. *A Pinprick of Light*. Brattleboro, Vermont: The Stephen Greene Press, 1974.

Chapman, Gerard. *The Gentleman Burglar and Other Favorites*. Great Barrington, Massachusetts: Attic Revivals Press, 1994.

Jackson, Richard S. Jr. and Cornelia Brooke Gilder. *Houses of the Berkshires 1870-1930*. New York, New York: Acanthus Press, 2006.

Owens, Carole. *The Berkshire Cottages, A Vanishing Era*. Stockbridge, Massachusetts: Cottage Press, Inc., 1984.

Peattie, Roderick, ed. *The Berkshires: the Purple Hills*. New York, New York: The Vanguard Press, Inc., 1948.

Red Lion Inn. *A History of the Red Lion Inn*. Stockbridge, Massachusetts: Red Lion Inn, 1987.

Rooney, E. Ashley. *Berkshire Ghosts, Legends, and Lore*. Atglen, Pennsylvania: Schiffer Publishing, Ltd., 2007.

Schultz, Eric B and Michael Tougias. *King Philip's War*. Woodstock, Vermont: The Countrymen Press, 1999.

Sedgwick, Sarah Cabot and Christina Sedgwick Marquard. *Stockbridge 1739-1939*. Great Barrington, Massachusetts: The Berkshire Courier, 1939.

Skinner, Charles M. *Myths and Legends of Our Own Land — Volume 04: Tales of Puritan Land*. Detroit Michigan: Singing Tree Press, 1969.

Smith, Charles and Susan Smith. *Discover the Berkshires*. Guilford, Connecticut: The Globe Pequot Press, 2003.

Todd, Charles Burr. *In Olde Massachusetts*. New York, New York: the Grafton Press, 1971.

Vaughan, Alden T. ed. *New England Encounters: Indians and Euroamericans ca. 1600-1850*. Boston, Massachusetts: Northeastern University Press, 1999.

Vaughan, Alden T. and Edward W. Clark. *Puritans Among the Indians*. Cambridge, Massachusetts: The Belknap Press, 1981.

Williams, John. *The Redeemed Captive Returning to Zion*. Ann Arbor, Michigan: University Microfilms, Inc., 1966.

Yankee Magazine Staff. "Danger, Disaster, and Horrid Deeds." Dublin, New Hampshire: *Yankee Magazine*, 1974.

Articles and Internet

Christian History Institute. "John Sergeant and the Stockbridge Indians," 1999-2006

Durwin, Joe. "Bizarre Berkshires: Tales spooky and otherwise." 2004

Durwin, Joe. "These Mysterious Hills," 2006

Egleston, N. H. "Story of the Hoosac Tunnel" In *The Atlantic Monthly*. Vol. XLIX .1882.

Hanny, Carol. "Megaliths, caves and other interesting stuff!" Internet site

Howes, Marc. "The History of the Hoosac Tunnel." 2004 Internet

"In Tanglewood's Tent." *Time* Magazine. Aug. 16, 1937

"Model for the Frontier." *Time* Magazine. Friday, July 4, 1969

"Plumb's Hotel, in Stockbridge, Destroyed by Fire." *Pittsfield Sun*, (MA) Sept. 3, 1896. p. 2

Smith, Gary. Compiler, "Finding Aid for the Hoosac Tunnel Collection," at The North Adams Public Library. North Adams, Massachusetts. May 2003

Index

Ashley House, 8

Becket, Massachusetts, 95, 97-98
Belvoir Terrace, 40-41
Berkshire Botanical Garden, 35
Berkshire Museum, 65-66
Birchwood Inn, 6-7, 36, 104-105
Blantyre, 43-44
Brook Farm Inn, 53

Canyon Ranch Spa, 42-43
Charlemont, Massachusetts, 112-113
Chesterwood, 33-34
Church on the Hill, 38-39
Crane & Co., 65, 72, 92-93
Cranwell Resort, Spa and Golf Club, 47-48
Curtis Hotel, 51

Dalton, Massachusetts, 92 -93
Deerfield, Massachusetts, 105-107

Florida, Massachusetts, 118

Great Barrington, Massachusetts, 13-29, 39-40
Greenfield, Massachusetts, 103-105

Hancock Shaker Village, 89-91
Holmesdale, 77-78
Hoosac Tunnel, 118-119, 126

Jacob's Pillow Dance, 6, 98-99

Kripalu Center for Yoga and Health, 49-50

Lee, Massachusetts, 39, 95, 98-99
Lenox, Massachusetts, 5-6, 36
Lenox Club, 53-54

Maple House, 100-101
MASS MoCA, 6, 120
Massachusetts Department of Conservation and Recreation, Division of State Parks and Recreation, 123

Millers Falls, Massachusetts, 103
Mission House, 25-26
Mohawk Trail State Forest, 115
Monument Mountain, 17-21
Mountain Washington State Forest, 12
Mount Greylock, 114, 121-123
Museum of the Gilded Age, (see Ventfort Hall)

Naumkeag, 42
Norman Rockwell Museum, 32-34
North Adams, Massachusetts, 119-120

Pittsfield, Massachusetts, 39, 61- 91
Pittsfield Athenaeum Club, 65

Red Lion Inn, 27-29
Rowe, Massachusetts, 100-101

Savoy State Forest, 116
Searles Castle, 16-17
Shakespeare & Company, 6, 57
Shelburne Massachusetts, 108-109
Shelburne Falls, Massachusetts, 109-112
Sheffield, Massachusetts, 8-10
Stockbridge, Massachusetts, 6, 25-35
Tanglewood, 6, 58-60
The Mount, 46
Trustees of Reservations, 8, 10, 26
Turners Falls, Massachusetts, 102

Ventfort Hall, 44-46
Village Inn, 52

Westfield, Massachusetts, 5, 95,122
Wheatleigh, 50
William Cullen Bryant Homestead, 15

Zoar Outdoor, 111